GHOSTS OF
KING PHILIP'S WAR

GHOSTS OF
KING PHILIP'S WAR

THOMAS D'AGOSTINO AND ARLENE NICHOLSON

Published by Haunted America
A Division of The History Press
Charleston, SC
www.historypress.com

First published 2024

Manufactured in the United States

ISBN 9781467157520

Library of Congress Control Number: 2024935281

Notice: The information in this book is true and complete to the best of our knowledge. It is offered without guarantee on the part of the authors or The History Press. The authors and The History Press disclaim all liability in connection with the use of this book.

This book is dedicated to the memory of all who lost their lives in what we now call King Philip's War. May their tragic end be a lesson for the future of peace and compromise.

CONTENTS

Acknowledgements

Many thanks go out to Christopher Balzano; Matthew Moniz; Jim Ignasher; Tim Weisberg; Putnam Public Library; New England Historical Society; Foster Preservation Society; the late, great Kent Spottswood and his website Stone Wings (https://stonewings.wordpress.com); Mike Girard of Strange New England (https://strangenewengland.com), Black Tavern Historical Society; Greenville Public Library; Smith's Castle; Oliver House in Middleborough, Massachusetts; Chrissy Parrish, Randall Parrish; Courtney McInvale and the Seaside Shadows Haunted History Tours; Peter Muise of the *New England Folk Lore* blog (http://newenglandfolklore.blogspot.com); Kelly Pincins; and everyone else who was instrumental in the creation of this book and wishes to remain anonymous.

Introduction

From the moment the Separatists—or as we now know them, Pilgrims—landed on the shores of New England, they were watched closely from afar. The Indigenous people of the land had already met Europeans, resulting in the devastation of many tribes. This was not due to war but because of diseases that they had never experienced or had a chance to build immunity against. Not only were they cautious about further infection from the outsiders, but they were also not sure of their intentions in coming to this new land. Were they hostile? Did they seek war against them? At the same time, the Pilgrims were very cautious about the people they called Indians. Both sides would soon meet, and with the help of an English-speaking Indian named Samoset, the colonists would become acquainted with Ousamequin, chief sachem of the Wampanoag Confederacy and sachem of the Pokanoket tribe. Ousamequin was introduced as Massasoit, which means "Great Chief." Not knowing this, the colonists took it as his name and called him Massasoit from then on. Both sides became very friendly toward each other and created a treaty on March 22, 1621, that would be diligently upheld by Massasoit, William Bradford, Edward Winslow, John Carver, Stephen Hopkins and Myles Standish.

Unfortunately, those who followed were not as peaceful as the original Pilgrims, and tensions formed between the two cultures. Massasoit had friction with the Pilgrims only when they refused to hand Squanto over to the Pokanokets, as Pokanokets believed he had, in some way, betrayed them. This disagreement was quickly resolved in 1623 when Massasoit, lying on his deathbed, was nursed back to health by Edward Winslow. The sachem would later state, "The English are my friends and love me....I will never forget their kindness."

By the time King Philip's War broke out, most of those peaceful and friendly allies were long gone, and the enmity between the colonists and the Indigenous people reached a boiling point that would set off a call for war. This war would prove to be the bloodiest and most brutal per capita ever fought on U.S. soil. Whole villages were raided and burned on both sides, and innocent men, women and children were mercilessly slaughtered. There were no rules of war or engagement among the people who fought. The conflict lasted from 1675 to 1676, when the English finally eradicated the main enemy antagonists, but many more rebellious skirmishes took place before the Treaty of Casco Bay was signed in 1678. This treaty was still largely ignored by the English, and subsequent small conflicts took more lives as a result. Even after the war ended, attacks continued in northern New England and later took on another form when the French sided with the Indigenous tribes, raiding English towns, killing or taking their inhabitants prisoner.

This brutal slaying of innocent people over several decades left an indelible scar on the land and atmosphere that comes to life to this day, occasionally reminding those who witness the paranormal encounters that the ghosts of King Philip's War and its aftermath will forever be at unrest. Tim Weisberg of *Spooky Southcoast* radio said it perfectly in an interview with the *Standard Times*'s Southcoast Today section when he stated,

> *The entire region was one big bloody battlefield and giant burial ground which basically means anyone's home could have been built on what was once an ancient burial ground.*

Tim Weisberg was spot on. Since the first European settlers arrived, the graves of the Indigenous peoples were desecrated for the treasures within. By the time the Puritans settled in Plymouth, it was understood that disturbing the local burial plots would worsen the relationship between them and the local tribes. One scouting party accidentally uncovered a grave, then quickly reburied the remains out of respect. Such respectful gestures were short-lived, however, as the English found out that the Natives buried their caches of corn for safekeeping, and therefore, any place that looked like a burial plot could contain food for the starving newcomers.

An illustration of the attempted burning of a fortified house during the war. *Public domain, from authors' collection.*

The disinterment of Native burials would spread as farms and towns sprang up everywhere, displacing the remains of the Indigenous and, at the same time, wiping out their history to a certain extent. The robbing of Indigenous graves continued into the nineteenth century, when hobbyists, collectors, anthropologists and archaeologists dug up the sites for collections of the bones and artifacts within the graves. Some of these remains were sent for study, while others ended up in private collections or museums. It was not until 1906 that Congress passed the Antiquities Act, making it illegal to perform unauthorized digs on federal land. The law did little to stop the looting on private property.

An old burial lot near Fort Ninigret in Charlestown, Rhode Island, met the same fate in the mid-twentieth century. Although a deed to the property filed in Providence on April 26, 1937, stated that the "Old Burial Indian Ground" was not to be improved on or destroyed, the markers were removed when a home was built on the land and a clump of bushes was planted over the graves.

Among these graves was that of Prince George, son of Ninigret, who was the chief of the Niantics. George was buried with about twenty other warriors. Further laws were passed in the 1960s and 1970s regarding illegal exhumations of Indigenous burials, but they did not require the return of any ancestral remains.

The Native American Graves Protection and Repatriation Act was passed in 1990, requiring universities, museums and other institutions to return any ancestral remains to their descendants. The law also made it illegal to sell remains or any stolen artifacts. How many have been returned compared to how many were taken over the centuries is still unknown.

In the pages of this book, you'll find many places you can visit and take in some of the most important history lessons this nation has to offer. Many are still inhabited by the ghosts and spirits of those who suffered at the hands of their enemies. Others, though not necessarily haunted, are still rich with legend and folklore—thus their significance in this book. The pages that follow will captivate and inform the reader about a mostly forgotten war and its accompanying legends and haunts. Whether you are visiting for the history or the haunts, one thing is assured: you will walk away with an experience you will never forget, both in your heart and in your mind.

WHO WAS KING PHILIP?

Metacom (Metacomet), born in 1640, was the second son of Massasoit (circa 1580–1661), chief sachem of the Wampanoag Confederacy and sachem of the Pokanokets. Massasoit had three sons, Wamsutta, Metacom and Sonkanuchoo, and two daughters, Amie and Sarah. Wamsutta and Metacom married the daughters of the Pocasset sachem Corbitant. Wamsutta married Weetamoo, and Metacom gave his hand to Wootonekanuske. Metacom, by then named Philip, had a son from her.

On the death of their father in 1661, Wamsutta and Metacom traveled to Plymouth and asked the Pilgrims to give them English names so they might better relate to their English neighbors. Their chosen names were Alexander and Philip, respectively. Wamsutta became the sachem for his people but did not maintain the diplomacy toward the original colonists his father spent decades preserving. He made an alliance with the Connecticut Colony, causing friction between him and the Plymouth Colony.

In 1662, Wamsutta (born in 1634), barely one year into his reign, was called to Plymouth to answer charges of illegal land sales negotiated without the consent of the Plymouth Colony. On his return home, he mysteriously died, and suspicions ran high that he may have been poisoned by the English. Philip was now chief sachem, yet he never again trusted the English, believing they were responsible for his brother's death. Soon after the death of Wamsutta, a fence was built across a stretch of land in Bristol from Warren to the Kickemuit River to demarcate the boundary between the Natives and the English. The deputy governor of the Plymouth Colony at the time was Josiah Winslow, son of Edward Winslow. He saw the Natives as obstacles that needed to be removed to make way for English growth in the New World.

It had become obvious to both sides that the death of Massasoit was basically the death of the treaty that had held the two cultures in peace for decades. With new leadership on both sides, tensions grew even more. The English encroached further onto Native lands without permission or compensation. The colonial government was unsympathetic toward the situation. Philip's faith in the English became depleted, and for the next several years, he barely tolerated their presence, wishing them gone from his native land.

It was in 1671 that Philip signed a pact of allegiance with the colonies. In his book *A Brief History of the War with the Indians in New-England*, Increase Mather included the public document, which is reproduced below:

Taunton, Apr. 10th, 1671

Whereas my Father, my Brother, and my self have formerly submitted our selves and our people unto the Kings Majesty of England, and to this Colony of New-Plymouth, by solemn Covenant under our Hand; but I having of late through my indiscretion, and the naughtiness of my heart violated and broken this my Covenant with my friends by taking up Arms, with evill intent against them, and that groundlessly; I being now deeply sensible of my unfaithfulness and folly, do desire at this time solemnly to renew my Covenant with my ancient Friends, and my Fathers friends above mentioned, and doe desire this may testifie to the world against me, if ever I shall again fail in my faithfullness towards them (that I have now and at all times found so kind to me) or any other of the English Colonyes; and as a reall Pledge of my true intentions, for the future to be faithfull and friendly, I doe freely ingage to resign up onto the Government of New-Plymouth, all my English Armes to be kept by them for their security, so long as they shall see reason. For true performance of the Premises I have hereunto set my hand together with the rest of my Council.

In the Presence of
William Davis.
William Hudson.
Thomas Brattle.

The Mark of Philip chief Sachem of Pocanoket.
The Mark of Tavoser.
The Mark of Capt. Wisposke.
The Mark of Woonkaponehunt.
The Mark of Nimrod.

It is quite doubtful that Philip and his council even cared what the pledge of allegiance stated, for the people Philip represented were being driven further and further from their own world and could not survive much longer with the English taking everything they had.

The colonists cleared forests, driving away the wild animals and killing the plants that were critical to the Natives' survival. Their livestock roamed the territory far outside the boundaries of their treaty. The Natives, in turn, had no choice but to eat the offending animals that laid waste to their food source. This caused the colonists to request that the culprits stand trial for theft. The new English rulers agreed that they no longer needed the Natives' help and the Natives now stood in the way of their expansion.

Tensions reached the boiling point when John Sassamon (Wussausmon), a Christian convert and interpreter for both sides, was found drowned with his neck broken in Assawompset Pond. He had traveled to Plymouth to warn the people of an impending attack being planned by King Philip but soon vanished. His body was discovered on January 29, 1675. Three of Philip's diplomatic advisers were arrested and charged with murder. On June 8 that year, the three were found guilty and executed. Philip became enraged, claiming they were innocent and the English had no right to execute any of his people. On June 11, the colonies, knowing Philip had gained an alliance with other chiefs, attempted to negotiate peace. Within days, the Wampanoags raided the town of Swansea. War had officially begun.

According to the *Pictorial History of King Philip's War*, by Daniel Strock Jr., the quarrels over land and subsequent starvation of Philip's people, along with the death of Sassamon, were among the main catalysts that led to war between Philip and the colonists.

PHILIP. *KING* of Mount Hope.

King Philip (Metacom). *Public domain, from authors' collection.*

A second cause of the war was the frequent demands of the settlers for the purchase of his lands. Philip was too wise not to discover that if these continued, he would not have a home in all the territories which his father had governed. From a period long before the death of Massasoit, until 1671, no year passed in which large tracts were not obtained by the settlers.

As their land was scooped up by the ever-growing English population, the Natives were forced to become increasingly dependent on the English for goods, weapons and food. What little resources in the land they had left grew scarce, putting the Natives in a situation where tribal leaders had little choice but to acknowledge the English as their authority.

Philip traveled about during the campaign hailing his forces for their attempt to rid their land of the English. In the end, it was one of his own, converted to Christianity, who would put an end to his life and the war. When Philip returned to his camp at Mount Hope, he was betrayed by a former counselor, John Alderman, who led Captain Benjamin Church into Philip's camp. When Philip ran to attack one of Church's men during the raid on the camp, Alderman shot him. His corpse was beheaded with a sword. It was then quartered with a hatchet and its hands cut off. Church gave Philip's head and scarred hand to Alderman as a trophy. Alderman carried them around in a bucket of rum, charging people to see the spoils of victory, until he finally sold them to the Plymouth Colony for thirty shillings. The head remained on a pole outside the fort in Plymouth for over a quarter of a century.

Philip's wife and son were sold into slavery, and Weetamoo, who had commanded her own force, was killed and mutilated, her head displayed at the Taunton colony. Philip's headdress and belt were sent to England as a gift to the king but never made it there. To this day, the search for the belt and headdress continues.

THE WAR

This section will detail many of the events that took place during the war. Any other places where legends and haunts may reside will be found in the subsequent sections. This section is intended to help the reader gain an understanding of the intensity of the brutal conflict and its consequences for the history of the region. It is necessary to include the incidents that transpired during the war in order to gain a better insight into why so many places still harbor the ghosts and spirits that came out of King Philip's War.

It must be noted that the average soldier of the time was not necessarily highly trained for battle. These were common folk, in most cases, who were forced by the war being waged on them to take defensive action. In many cases, training was short, and then the troops were off to protect their kith and kin. The following paragraphs briefly describe the weaponry and tactics that both sides favored in the conflict.

Early settlers brought mostly iron weapons from Europe. Knives, axes and matchlock muskets were used for everyday tasks as well as defense in the New World. Although the bow and arrow was still in use in the Old World, the art of archery was considered a skill for the upper crust and not so much for the common folk who had sailed so many miles to brave the harsh new land. Matchlock muskets were common but would prove useless in the dense forest and brush. The matchlock, being several feet long and weighing about twenty pounds, was a very cumbersome weapon, especially when traveling a long distance. Its efficiency was also questioned, as it needed a "match," or long wick, that was ignited and burned slowly while the gun was in use. Constant adjustments to the wick and loading of the powder, an effective range of just fifty yards, the inability to fire in damp or wet weather and the necessity of some sort of brace to rest the end of the gun on—these were just a few of the drawbacks of this rifle in the New World. It still fared better than the bow and arrow as far as power was concerned, but when cover and stealth were necessary, if the glow from the match did not give the shooter away, the smell of the wick usually did. The first settlers wore armor, but that proved to be inhibiting during forest warfare. The armor mostly consisted of a corselet (a piece of armor covering the trunk of the body); a breastplate; thigh, groin and neck protection; and a helmet. Though much skimpier than the suits of armor that the knights of old wore, all this was still bulky and slowed the wearer down considerably. It would later be discarded, mostly because the Indigenous people also possessed plenty of guns by the time the war broke out. Arrows could not pierce armor as easily as a lead ball, and the settlers soon learned they could dodge arrows if they saw them coming. As more tribes obtained guns, the armor and arrows saw less and less use in the wild thickets of New England.

The flintlock soon replaced the matchlock as a weapon of choice. The flintlock contained a piece of flint that struck a metal part called a frizzen when the trigger was pulled. This created a spark that lit the powder in the pan, sending the flame through a small hole in the barrel and lighting the powder there. The powder tray could also be covered, making it usable in wet or damp weather.

In 1646, the Plymouth Colony required every town to have at least two flintlocks per thirty men. At first, the bow and arrow was more efficient than the musket for New England terrain. New England Indians immediately began obtaining flintlock rifles and carbines through trading with the French, Dutch and English. Knowing that the Natives were more competent hunters in the new land, the settlers were more than happy to trade their firearms for food and the ever-necessary fur for warm clothing. The Indigenous peoples, at the same time, were more than happy to trade furs and wampum for firearms, which they became more proficient at using than the average colonist. The English did not think that there would be any risks per se in trading guns to the Native people, who could more efficiently hunt for food with the more modern firearm as opposed to the archaic bow and arrow. Unfortunately, this mindset would prove to be a major chink in their plans, putting them at a disadvantage, as the playing field would be more level in terms of firepower by the time the war broke out.

The perennial and indispensable swords that the English carried were also too cumbersome for woodland combat. The most effective weapons during the war were the flintlock, the hatchet and the knife, as much of the fighting would be hand-to-hand combat, rendering anything but close-quarter weaponry useless. The hatchet and the knife were everyday tools for both sides, so it was common for every person to have one or both. The Natives also used war clubs custom-designed to suit the carrier's taste or tribal representation. Strangely, bows were not used much during the war. At one point, the Native people of New England almost completely lost the art of bow hunting due to their reliance on flintlocks.

Colonists settling in New England came from a completely different way of doing battle. They were used to conducting warfare in the open with an all-out melee, whereas the Indigenous peoples' way was more like guerrilla warfare. Hand-to-hand combat and the element of surprise were among the main tactics of warfare the European colonists were not familiar with or experienced in. Ambushes were something the Native warriors relied on and, in many cases, were very successful at. These were frequently carried out in places where steep hills, cliffs, marshes, rivers, lakes and other natural features inhibited the English from being able to readily escape the fury. Such tactics were unfamiliar to the English, who fell prey to them several times during Philip's War. During the French and Indian War, several decades later, Major Robert Rogers, leader of the famous Rogers' Rangers, employed such Native tactics in his form of fighting with great success. In fact, he wrote a manual based on the Native American guerrilla-style fighting and his own innovative combat techniques called *The 28 Rules of Ranging*, which is still being used by the U.S. Army today.

Several factors brought on King Philip's War. For the most part, the main cause was the ill-treatment of the Native Americans by the ruling powers of the Plymouth Colony after the deaths of Massasoit and Edward Winslow. Thomas Prence, the twelfth governor of the Plymouth Colony, remained fair and humane to the Native people. On Prence's death in 1673 at the age of seventy-three, Josiah Winslow, son of Edward Winslow, the same man who saved Massasoit's life, became governor.

Winslow was unsympathetic toward the Natives and became an opportunist, scooping up as much of their lands as he could. Whenever his practices were called illegal, he used his position to rewrite the laws to suit his wants. Winslow took more and more land from the Indigenous peoples, sometimes calling on debts accrued before they were due or forcing the debtor to mortgage or hand over land. The tribes, without hunting and fishing grounds, began to starve. As the relationship between the English and the Indigenous peoples further deteriorated, competition for land and resources increased. Philip decided it was time to drive the English out of the region once and for all.

He began meeting with tributary chiefs for aid in driving the English from the region. Much of the uprising plans were overheard by John Sassamon, an interpreter and liaison between the English and the Natives. Sassamon ran to Plymouth to warn Winslow about the potential uprising, but his report was dismissed as mere folly. Shortly after, Sassamon's body was found in the ice of Assawompset Pond in Middleborough, Massachusetts. As mentioned in the previous section, three of Philip's closest advisers were executed for the murder, and the seeds of war began to sprout. (See the Assawompset Pond story that follows for more details.) In retaliation for the executions, English farms were raided, cattle shot, corn stolen, houses robbed while the villagers were at church and outbuildings burned.

The war began and ended within the limits of Rehoboth but was not confined to that area. Guerrilla raids by Native American tribes and reprisals by the colonists spread all over New England, especially in Massachusetts, Rhode Island and eastern Connecticut. The Indians, at the start of the war, plundered homes but offered no violence to settlers they encountered on the way to their raids as they, in a superstitious way, felt the side to shed first blood would ultimately be the loser of the conflict. This practice of not harming the settlers would turn very quickly after one of their raiders was killed during an attack.

On June 24, 1675, a band of Philip's warriors attacked the village of Swansea (Swanzy) on the Sabbath. In his *Brief History of the War with the Indians in New-England,* Increase Mather wrote,

> *June. 24. (Midsummer-day) was appointed and attended as a day of solemn Humiliation throughout the Colony, by fasting and prayer, to intreat the Lord to give success to the present expedition respecting the Enemy. At the conclusion of that day of Humiliation, as soon as ever the people in Swanzy were come from the place where they had been praying together, the Indians discharged a volley of shot whereby they killed one man & wounded others. Two men were sent to call a Surgeon for the relief of the wounded, but the Indians killed them by the way: and in another part of the town six men were killed, so that there were nine english men murthered this day.*
>
> *Thus did the War begin, this being the first english blood that was spilt by the Indians in an hostile way.*

Several days later, June 26–29, the Wampanoags attacked the towns of Rehoboth and Taunton, Massachusetts. These were, at the time, hinterland towns on the edge of colonial settlement. On July 8–9, they stormed into Middleborough, Massachusetts, burning most of the homes and driving the English from the settlement. They then turned their destructive force toward Dartmouth, Massachusetts, burning about three dozen homes and killing some of their inhabitants. The English had marched to Mount Hope, where Philip's main base camp was, but found he had already departed for Pocasset, Massachusetts, with plans for further attacks.

The Nipmucks, in turn, attacked settlements in their own territory. On July 14, they made ruin of Mendon, Massachusetts, killing six English. In less than a month, English settlements were already being burned, and many tribes were in full-fledged war with the colonies. Among the tribes that joined Philip and his Wampanoags in his quest to rid the region of the English were the Nipmucks, Pocumtucks, Mohegans, Mohawks and, later, the Narragansetts. The Mohegans had pledged their support for the English but later sided with Philip when they proved to be treated no better in the end. The Narragansetts, who had wished to stay neutral throughout the conflict, were literally burned out of their winter camp and forced to take up arms against their former English friends.

Wheeler's Surprise monument on West Road in New Braintree, Massachusetts. *Photo courtesy of Arlene Nicholson.*

On July 19, Philip was at Pocasset Swamp with his warriors when the Massachusetts and Plymouth troops came upon a few of his scouts. Two of the warriors were killed, and the third was pursued into the swamp, where he managed to escape. Philip and his army fled the swamp on rafts, entering Nipmuck territory. This would be pivotal, as the Nipmucks wanted to remain neutral for the rest of the war.

In early August, the Natives destroyed the colony of Quabaug near Brookfield. This was also the area of present-day New Braintree where "Wheeler's Surprise" took place. The Nipmucks ambushed Captain Thomas Wheeler and Captain Edward Hutchinson's troops. A meeting was arranged between the captains and the Nipmucks on a plain a few miles from Brookfield.

When the English arrived, they found no Nipmucks in sight. Instead of turning back, they decided to move forward and encountered a narrow path between a steep hill and a swamp. As the English bottlenecked into the trail, they were met with an ambush by what Wheeler described as two hundred or more men. In his narrative, Captain Wheeler recounted the following:

> *The said perfidious Indians sent out their shot upon us as a shower of hail…. We seeing ourselves so beset, and not having room to fight, endeavored*

to fly for the safety of our lives. They fired violently out of the swamp, and from behind the bushes on the hillside, wounding me sorely.

In the end, both Wheeler and Hutchinson were wounded; Captain Hutchinson died from his wounds several days later in Marlboro, Massachusetts. Eight other men were killed and several wounded. The remainder of the company made it to the home of Jonathan Ayres, who was killed during the ambush. There they, along with others from Brookfield, fortified themselves in preparation for another attack. Two hours later, the Nipmucks swarmed the town; they laid siege to the garrison for two days. The Indians continued a hail of gunfire on the home and shouted at the English. One of the English attempted to escape past the warriors to secure provisions from his home. He was found on the way back and beheaded. After tossing his head around, the Indians placed it on a pole in front of the door of the house in plain sight.

The Indians shot flaming arrows onto the roof, but the occupants were able to punch holes in the roof and put them out. The building was set on fire but, with much difficulty, was also extinguished. Another attempt to set the house on fire failed when heavy showers fell, making a cart full of flax,

The former Ayres Tavern, used as a garrison against the enemy, has stood the test of centuries. *Photo courtesy of Arlene Nicholson.*

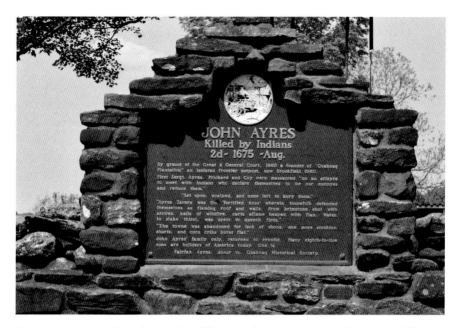

Monument in front of the former Ayres Tavern and garrison, now a private home. *Photo courtesy of Arlene Nicholson.*

hay and wood the Indians intended to use as a firebomb impossible to light. The village meetinghouse was so close to the Ayres home turned garrison that the English could hear the warriors inside mocking their psalms and taunting them about how their god was doing nothing for them at that point.

Some of the warriors occupied a vantage point on a hill across from the garrison where a great boulder sat. Behind that boulder, they were able to take shelter and spy on the goings-on in the hideout. After three nights, Major Willard and his men arrived, fighting alongside whoever was still alive in the garrison. The Indians withdrew from the area, burning as much of Brookfield, now abandoned, as they could and feeling confident they had scored a major victory. To this day, that boulder is known as Indian Rock. It sits prominently on a rise in a field across from the Ayres homestead, now called Indian Rock Farm. The area on Foster Hill Road in New Braintree is marked with stone monuments that tell of the deadly skirmish. The farm and rock are on private property but can be viewed from the road. Just being there gives one the feeling of tragedy. Whether the place is haunted has not been publicly noted, but be assured that an eternal lingering energy is felt while standing among the stone monuments marking where the event happened.

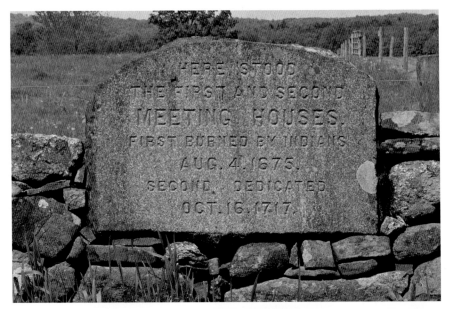

This page, top: Marker for the former meetinghouse at Indian Rock Farm where the warriors mocked the English during the siege of the Ayres garrison. *Photo courtesy of Arlene Nicholson.*

This page, bottom: Indian Rock in the field at Indian Rock Farm where the Nipmuck warriors held fast during the raid of the garrison. *Photo courtesy of Arlene Nicholson.*

Opposite: Old well on the Indian Rock farm across the street from the former garrison. The English could not reach it during the raid. *Photo courtesy of Arlene Nicholson.*

On September 28, 1675, a force of several hundred Pocumtuck, Nipmuck and Wampanoag warriors ambushed and killed fifty-nine teamsters (wagoneers who drove carts pulled by a team of oxen) and militia at the Battle of Bloody Brook. The Narragansett tribe remained neutral but agreed to take in noncombatants: women, children and the wounded. Josiah Winslow accused them of aiding the enemy and, on December 19, 1675, led an attack on their stronghold, slaughtering over six hundred Narragansetts as well as the women, children and injured of other tribes. The Narragansetts then joined the war on Philip's side. (See later chapters for accounts of these haunted places.)

One of the most noted raids by the Native American forces was the attack on and burning of Lancaster, Massachusetts, which took place on February 10, 1676. A raiding party of Narragansett, Nipmuck and Wampanoag warriors attacked the settlement at sunrise, first burning the entry bridge so that any English forces could not easily come to the rescue. The account is well documented by Mary Rowlandson in her book *The Narrative of the Captivity and Restoration of Mrs. Mary Rowlandson*. In the first paragraphs, she wrote:

On the tenth of February 1676 came the Indians with vast numbers upon Lancaster: their first coming was about sun rising; hearing the noise of some guns, we looked out; several houses were burning, and the smoke ascended to heaven. There were five persons taken in one house, the father, and the mother and a sucking child they knocked on the head; the other two they took and carried away alive. There were two others, who being out of their garrison upon some occasion were set upon; one was knocked on the head, the other escaped: another their was who running among was shot and wounded, and fell down; he begged for his life, promising them money (as they told me) but they would not hearken to him but knocked him in the head....Thus the numerous wretches went on, burning, and destroying before them.

"Knocked on the head" was a phrase the English used for being dispatched with a hatchet to the head. It was a less brutal term than *dispatched* or *killed* for a very barbarous act of murder. The raiding party burned the Rowlandson home, which was also being used as a garrison. Mary Rowlandson grabbed some of her own and her sister's children and ran for the door, but as soon as she opened it, the raiders

shot so thick, the bullets rattled against the house, as if one had taken a handful of stones and threw them....We had six stout dogs belonging to our garrison but none of them would stir, though another time, if any Indian had come to the door, they were ready to fly upon him and tear him down.

During the raid, Mary was shot in the side and her daughter Sarah was shot in the hand. Sarah died at age six while in captivity in present-day Hardwick. Mary's other two children taken in the raid were sold as property. Mary's narrative is very graphic and precise, offering an indispensable wealth of knowledge about the raid of Lancaster and her travels with the enemy before she was ransomed and released at Redemption Rock. (See Mary's story in a later section.)

On May 19, 1676, in present-day Gill, Massachusetts, a massacre took place that still reverberates in the annals of history as a most heinous act by the English during the war. Captain William Turner and about 160 ill-trained soldiers arrived in present-day Gill, where they attacked an Indian encampment, Peskeompskut, filled with women, children and the elderly. This camp along the Connecticut River was known as an established annual fishing camp of the Algonquin people. The war had displaced members of many other tribes who were also camped there at the time of the raid. An estimated more than two hundred women and children were killed in the attack. The Algonquin warriors, camped about half a mile away, heard the melee and counterattacked.

The tribe set ambushes in areas where Turner's men were retreating. Captain Turner and thirty-seven of his men were killed during the retreat, and an unknown number were wounded. The event was considered an act of genocide. In Mather's *Brief History of the War with the Indians in New-England*, he describes it as a "great and notable slaughter." The site is now on the National Register of Historic Places.

The war came to a speedy end between August and September 1676. Philip had retreated to his home at Mount Hope. A Sakonnet named John Alderman offered to guide Captain Benjamin Church to the place where Philip and his men were hiding out. Captain Church anticipated that Philip's band would retreat into the swamp once the signal was given to attack. He placed his men in ambush behind trees, one Indian and one Englishman to each tree. Philip, at this time, was relating to one of his comrades a dream he had the previous night (see the section called "King Philip's Dream") in which he was placed in the hands of the enemy; it seemed to him to presage his speedy end.

At that moment, one of Philip's men happened to glance toward the spot where two of Church's men were hiding. The Englishman, who saw the glance and thought he had been discovered, fired at once at the enemy. The Pokanoket band, just as Church predicted, made haste into the swamp to effect their escape. Philip, on the contrary, rushed toward his assailants. The Englishman's gun misfired, but Alderman's bullet went right through Philip's heart, killing him instantly.

It was estimated that about 800 settlers and about 3,000 Indigenous people were killed during the war. Many more were enslaved or became refugees. An estimated casualty count per 100,000 yielded 15,000 Native Americans and 1,538 English. For all its brutality, the Civil War came in at 857 per 100,000. The numbers may not be exact, but they reflect the brutality of the conflict, given that the population of people settled in New England was much less than it is at present. Fifty-two of the ninety English towns were attacked, twenty-five were pillaged and seventeen burned to the ground. The major battles of the conflict that took place in Massachusetts were in Plymouth, Scituate, Boston, Pocasset, Dartmouth, Bridgewater, Swansea, Fall River, Marlborough, Sudbury, Lancaster, Brookfield, New Braintree, Turner's Falls, Hadley, Rehoboth, Taunton, Springfield, Deerfield, Great Barrington, North Hampton, Hatfield, Pennacook, Mendon, Medford, Groton and Middleborough. In Rhode Island, attacks took place on Smithfield (now North Smithfield), Central Falls, Mount Hope, South Kingstown, Tiverton, Warwick and Providence. Connecticut saw major fighting in Simsbury on March 26, 1676. It is reported that Philip sat in a cave on Avon Mountain just outside of town and watched as the settlement burned. Connecticut tried to stay friendly or as neutral as possible in the conflict. New Hampshire had a few raids in Ossipee.

Maine saw raids mostly in the coastal towns of Scarborough, Arrowsik, Pemequid, Wells, York and Woolrich. The Pine Tree State's fishing industry was almost completely eradicated by the enemy's flotilla, which consisted of about a dozen boats taken by the Indians. The fishermen were not well equipped for battle, and many were easily killed or taken prisoner. The death toll in Maine by the time the treaty was signed was approximately four hundred settlers and between one hundred and two hundred Indigenous people. Other battles and ambushes took place in wooded areas or places on the outskirts of towns. The toll of the war was monumental on both sides, making it the bloodiest war per capita in U.S. history.

Although the war officially ended in 1676 with the death of King Philip, hostilities continued in northern New England well into 1678 until the Treaty of Casco was signed on August 12, 1678, in New Casco, now Falmouth, Maine. Among the conditions of the treaty: the English had to pay rent to the Wabanakis for settling on their land and give one peck of corn from each family per year. In turn, the English were given back farmland taken by the tribes in the war. The English agreed to leave the Penobscots alone. The Wabanaki agreed to recognize English property but retained sovereignty over the territory of Maine. All captives were returned to their rightful homes. Unfortunately, the English never kept their word, as the settlers refused to obey the conditions of the treaty.

On April 7, 1677, several men were slain by the Indians near York, Maine, while working but a few miles from the town. On April 29, an Indian presented himself near Wells, Maine—on purpose, as it would later prove, to draw out some of the English from the garrison into a trap. Lieutenant Benjamin Swett, commander of the garrison at the time, had left to assist in securing the town of Wells. He sent several of his soldiers to scout out the area and then lie in wait at a convenient place until they sighted the enemy. While they were searching, they fell into an ambush, in which two of the men were shot down and a third one mortally wounded.

The hostilities drew much fear and concern from the settlers, as no one knew when they were going to be attacked. Fortifications and garrisons were the only comforts the English had as a measure of safety. When the French became involved, the game changed, and for another few decades, New

England towns lived in constant fear of attack, especially the more northerly towns that were closer to the Canadian border.

The attacks continued, even after another treaty was signed on June 20, 1703. The Wabanaki disavowed any aid to the French, but this would quickly change, as you will read in the following pages. The French and Indian raids on English settlements were a carryover from King Philip's War. The French knew they had an ally in the Indians, and both were bitter enemies of the English.

The legends, haunts and folklore that follow have become associated with King Philip's War and the French and Indian attacks on English settlements shortly thereafter. The places described can be visited and even investigated, for the most part. Some may be on private property, so please respect the owner's rights and requests.

A BRIEF TIMELINE OF KING PHILIP'S WAR

JANUARY 29, 1675
John Sassamon is found murdered in Assawompset Pond.

JUNE 8, 1675
Sassamon's alleged assassins are executed in Plymouth.

JUNE 14–25, 1675
Rhode Island, Massachusetts and Plymouth Colonies try to negotiate a peaceful treaty with Philip and several other tribal chiefs.

JUNE 24, 1675
The Wampanoag Confederacy attacks Swansea, Massachusetts, effectively starting the historic war.

JUNE 26–29, 1675
The Wampanoags attack Rehoboth and Taunton, Massachusetts, while the Mohegans travel to Boston claiming their loyalty to the English and offering to side with them in the conflict.

July 8–9, 1675

The Wampanoags attack Middleborough and Dartmouth, Massachusetts.

July 14, 1675

The Nipmuck attack Mendon, Massachusetts.

July 15, 1675

The Narragansetts sign a peace treaty with the Connecticut Colony.

July 19, 1675

Philip temporarily takes refuge in Nipmuck territory, thus endangering the Nipmucks' neutrality in the conflict.

August 2–4, 1675

The Nipmucks attack and besiege Brookfield, Massachusetts.

August 13, 1675

Christian Indians are confined to their respective praying towns.

August 22, 1675

Seven colonists are killed in the Lancaster, Massachusetts raid.

September 1–2, 1675

Wampanoag and Nipmuck warriors attack Deerfield, Massachusetts, while Samuel Moseley and his men attack the village of Pennecook.

September 12, 1675

The Battle of Bloody Brook takes place, in which fifty-seven out of seventy-nine English are killed, prompting the abandonment of Deerfield, Squakeag and Brookfield.

September 18, 1675

Narragansetts sign a peace treaty in Boston. Massachusetts troops are ambushed near Northampton.

October 5, 1675

Pocumtucks destroy Springfield, Massachusetts, while Philip reportedly looks on from a hill nearby.

OCTOBER 13, 1675

Massachusetts orders all "Praying Indians" confined to Deer Island in Boston Harbor, where most of them die from lack of food, water and shelter.

OCTOBER 19, 1675

An attack on Hatfield, Massachusetts, is effectively repelled.

DECEMBER 19, 1675

The English attack the stronghold of the Narragansetts at Great Swamp in South Kingstown, Rhode Island, in the most brutal engagement of the war. Many are killed, including women and children.

JANUARY 1676

Philip travels to New York in hopes of having the Mohawks side with him. Instead, they attack him, driving him back to New England.

JANUARY 27, 1676

The Narragansetts attack Pawtuxet, a part of the Plymouth Bay Colony in Massachusetts.

FEBRUARY 10, 1676

Mary Rowlandson is taken captive during the Nipmuck raid on Lancaster. She later writes of her ordeal in a book that is in print to this day.

FEBRUARY 14, 1676

Philip and his warriors attack Northampton, Massachusetts.

FEBRUARY 21, 1676

The Nipmucks attack Medfield, Massachusetts.

MARCH 1, 1676

The Nipmucks attack Groton, Massachusetts.

MARCH 26, 1676

Three settlements—Longmeadow, Massachusetts; Marlborough, Massachusetts; and Simsbury, Connecticut—are attacked on the same day.

MARCH 27, 1676
Sudbury, Massachusetts, is attacked by Nipmuck warriors.

MARCH 28, 1676
Raiding parties attack Rehoboth, Massachusetts, where present-day
  Cumberland and Central Falls, Rhode Island are located. Almost every
  English soldier and friendly Indian soldier is massacred in what becomes
  known as Pierce's Fight.

MARCH 30, 1676
Providence Colony is destroyed. Roger Williams is told beforehand to
  vacate the colony, as the Indians have great respect for him.

APRIL 21, 1676
Sudbury, Massachusetts, is attacked again; this time, half the militia are
  casualties of the conflict.

MAY 2–3, 1676
Captive Mary Rowlandson is ransomed at a place now called Redemption
  Rock. The exchange takes place with Philip present, yet he refuses to
  consent to it.

MAY 19, 1676
In the Battle of Turner's Falls in Western Massachusetts, English forces
  surprise Indians camping near the falls, resulting in the killing of an
  estimated two to three hundred Indians.

MAY 30, 1676
Hatfield, Massachusetts, is attacked.

MAY 31, 1676
The remaining Praying Indians are taken from Deer Island and brought to
  Cambridge, Massachusetts.

JUNE 12, 1676
Another attack on Hadley is thwarted, by what is known as the "Angel of
  Hadley."

JUNE 19, 1676

Massachusetts promises amnesty for any Indian who surrenders into their authority.

JULY 2, 1676

The second battle of Nipsachuck Swamp in North Smithfield, Rhode Island, takes place. Major John Talcott and his men begin sweeping through Rhode Island and Connecticut, capturing large numbers of Natives and selling them into slavery to pay off debts incurred during the war. The Indian queen Quaiapen attempts to escape but drowns in the swamp.

JULY 11, 1676

Taunton, Massachusetts, is again attacked; this time, the attack is successfully repelled.

JULY 27, 1676

Roughly two hundred Nipmucks make their way to Boston to surrender to the authorities.

AUGUST 2, 1676

Captain Benjamin Church captures Philip's wife and son, then sells them into slavery.

AUGUST 6, 1676

Weetamoo, a Pocasset Wampanoag chief, drowns in the Taunton River while attempting her escape from the English. Her head is paraded around Taunton.

AUGUST 12, 1676

In the skirmish at Mount Hope, Rhode Island, an English soldier attempts to shoot Philip, but it is one of Philip's own, named John Alderman, who takes the fatal shot, effectively ending the war.

SEPTEMBER 19, 1676

Benjamin Church finally captures Chief Annawan at his hideout in the swamps of Rehoboth. Church is presented with Philip's belt and other ceremonial dress.

1676–1678

Hostilities continue throughout New England until the war is, by written agreement, concluded with the Treaty of Casco in Maine.

1678–1713

The French side with many of the tribes that were forced to flee to Canada. The alliance begins to attack English settlements, with devastating results. This is termed Queen Anne's War. Queen Anne's War eventually wound down, but not until the land was permanently scarred with the events that transpired for almost half a century.

CHAPTER 1

THE GHOSTS OF KING PHILIP'S WAR

ASSAWOMPSET POND (JOHN SASSAMON)

Assawompset Pond in Middleborough, Massachusetts, was the scene of a most hideous murder. This horrific deed was one of the main sparks that ignited the war between the New England Indigenous tribes and the English colonies. Assawompset Pond is the largest body of water in Massachusetts and was once a Wampanoag summer campsite. The name means "place of white stone." Archaeological digs in the late 1950s uncovered artifacts and a burial ground dating as far back as 2300 BC; the burial ground was subsequently excavated for more research into the history and culture of the Indigenous people of the area.

On January 29, 1675, in one area called Betty's Neck, the body of John Sassamon was found. A group of Algonquins stumbled upon Sassamon's body floating beneath the ice. At first, Sassamon's death was ruled an accident, but as time went by, authorities came to believe he was murdered.

Sassamon was a Praying Indian, having converted to Christianity with the help of missionary John Eliot. It was Eliot who also arranged for his education at Harvard University. Sassamon went back and forth between the English and the Wampanoags, translating and arranging deals and agreements between the two. When Sassamon learned of a plan to attack the colonies, he ran to Plymouth to warn Governor Winslow. Winslow took the intelligence with a grain of salt, sending Sassamon on his way. Shortly after, Sassamon was found murdered and thrown into the icy water.

Not long after Sassamon was found, another Native came forward with information about who the murderers were. He claimed that three of King Philip's advisers murdered the Praying Indian and threw his lifeless body into the water to hide their deed. The three accused were Tobias, Mattaschunanamoo and Wampapaquin, son of Tobias. They were arrested by the English, tried and sentenced to death. Tobias and Mattaschunanamoo were hanged, and Wampapaquin was later shot. The executions took place regardless of Philip's pleas of their innocence.

George Ellis and John Morris, authors of *King Philip's War*, documented a piece of testimony brought forth by the accused:

> The Indians claimed that Sassamon had been drowned while fishing and that the marks on his body were caused by contact with the ice. They declared that the informer who claimed to have been an eyewitness, "had gambled away his coat and, on its being returned and payment demanded, he had, in order to escape the debt, accused them of the murder knowing it would please the English and cause them to think him the better Christian."

The famous Reverend Cotton Mather wrote of an old supernatural way of telling if the accused parties were guilty. This was a common ritual used in those times called cruentation, ordeal of the touch or ordeal of the bier. The accused was brought to a courtroom before the murder victim and instructed to touch the body. If the body bled or exhibited any other unnatural signs when touched, it was thought to be God's way of saying that that accused was guilty. Tobias was brought forth to touch Sassamon's body, and according to Mather, the body began to bleed when he approached it. This sealed the three Wampanoags' fate, but the stains of the incident remain at the lake to this day.

Between the burial ground being disturbed and the murder of Sassamon, it is no wonder the area of Betty's Neck is haunted. Burial grounds are sacred, and disturbing them allegedly angers the spirits. Locals claim to see strange flickering lights in the woods by the pond where the camp was. Some have seen apparitions of Indians from long ago appear in the woods and then suddenly disappear right in front of them. Visitors often feel like the woods, or something in the woods, is watching them as they trek the trails. Perhaps the three advisers who were hanged by the English are among those who haunt the area that sealed their fate.

According to one account, a woman visiting the area heard her child talking to someone, yet no visible person was present. When she asked who

The murder of John Sassamon. *Public domain, from authors' collection.*

the child was speaking with, the youngster answered that "Conanchet" was talking about how he used to fish the waters there many years ago.

There are hiking trails, and fishing or boating are allowed but not swimming. Take a picnic basket and enjoy the scenery. Perhaps you may encounter one of the many that linger long after their time on earth as a mortal has passed. Take Betty's Neck Road off Route 44 and hit the trails.

THE GHOST HEADS OF THE KICKEMUIT RIVER

The Kickemuit River once was the scene of another ghastly event, signaling the first official bloodshed of King Philip's War. As one looks across the banks of the Kickemuit River, cattails sit along the shores like a scene from a still-life painting. Suddenly, a terrifying image of eight severed heads appears, floating along the tree line near the river.

On June 20, 1675, tensions between Philip and the colonists had reached the boiling point. The ill feeling became a bloody reality when a band of Pokanoket warriors attacked the settlement of Swansea along the banks of

Kickemuit River, where the severed heads of eight colonists are still seen. *Photo courtesy of Arlene Nicholson.*

the Kickemuit River. They looted and vandalized several homes, burning two to the ground. Three days later, the Pokanokets returned during the day of humiliation, or Sabbath, to ransack and burn more houses. John Salisbury shot and wounded one of the Indians as they retreated.

The following day, the band returned to exact revenge for the shooting. King Philip's warriors captured and killed John Salisbury along with six other colonists near Swazey Corner during the struggle. Two other men were ambushed and killed as they ran to the nearby settlements for help. In his book *A Narrative of the Causes Which Led to Philip's Indian War, of 1675 and 1676* (rendered below in modern English) John Easton relates,

In this time Indians fell a pilfering some houses the English had left, and an old man and a lad going to one of these houses did see three Indians run out thereof. The old man bid the young man shoot; so he did, and an Indian fell down but got away again. It is reported some Indians came to the garrison, asked why they shot the Indian. They asked whether he was dead. The Indians said "Yea." A English lad said it was no matter. The men endeavored to inform them it was but an idle lad's words, but the Indians in haste went away and did not hearken to them. The next day, the lad that shot the Indian and his father, and six English men were killed so the war begun with Philip.

On the evening of June 29, Major Thomas Savage along with his troops assembled at Swansea with another force totaling over five hundred men. Some proceeded toward Mount Hope in hopes of confronting Philip but came upon a ghastly sight, related in William Hubbard's *The History of the Indian Wars in New England Volume I*:

> *After they had marched about a Mile and Half, they passed by some Houses newly burned: not far off one of them they found a Bible newly torn, and the Leaves scattered about by the Enemy in Hatred of our Religion therein revealed; two or three Miles further they came up with some Heads, Scalps, and Hands cut off from the Bodies of some of the English, and stuck upon Poles near the Highway.*

As a sign of victory and a warning to the English that war was coming, the severed heads and hands of the murdered colonists were placed on the banks of the river near the highway, mounted on long poles with gruesome smiles pulled across their faces. This was a clear message to Governor Winslow and the colonies that the Natives would no longer put up with their land being

Swazey Corner, where the English were ambushed by the Indians at the start of the war. *Photo courtesy of Arlene Nicholson.*

taken and their people being mistreated. War broke out within days, and New England would never be the same, both historically and ethereally. The conflict would eventually end, but the innocent colonists who died that day never left the spot where their heads were hung for all to see.

Several times a year, residents of Warren witness eight disembodied heads floating above the shore of the river. The ghostly heads are also seen about the trees glowing in the twilight hours of early evening. Sometimes they are witnessed on poles in the ground at the edge of the water near the bridge that crosses the river at Route 136. Either way, it is a grim sight to behold. Witnesses who have seen them say the heads have macabre smiles stretched across them. When you visit the Kickemuit River, take a stroll along the banks. You may find that you are being watched by eight glowing faces with hideous smiles extended across their faces, staring down at you wondering if you are friend or foe.

The Kickemuit River runs through the center of Warren. Take Interstate Route 195 East to Route 114 East. Bear left where Routes 114 and 103 split. Take Route 136 South off Route 103.

SAKONNET RIVER

The Sakonnet River is a saltwater strait that separates Rhode (Aquidneck) Island from the mainland to the east. The span of the waterway is approximately fourteen miles, flowing from Mount Hope Bay to Rhode Island Sound. The name Sakonnet, translated to English, means "haunt of the wild black goose." Archaeological expeditions along the river revealed that the area was extensively inhabited by Indigenous peoples during prehistoric and early historic times. Artifacts from several ancient tribes were uncovered during subsequent digs.

With such an ancient history, it is no wonder the river holds some remnants of the past. Phantom canoes carrying their ghostly passengers have been witnessed by many locals and visitors alike. Those who witness the phenomenon watch in awe while the canoes glide silently on the surface of the water. The oars create no wake or swirl as they dip into the water and then rise back out for another ethereal revolution. When the observers call out to the occupants in the canoes, both people and vessels vanish. In 1984, three residents of the area witnessed a ghostly canoe and its occupants, but one more strange incident transpired. The people in the canoe threw their arms into the air as if performing a ritual or summoning a higher power. A few moments later, the water around the canoe began glowing a bright green. Within moments of this strange otherworldly occurrence, the canoe and its occupants were gone.

No one knows exactly who the Natives were or why they appear. One theory is that they may be a remnant of King Philip's War recreating some sort of curse that failed to work on the English back then. Perhaps they are still trying to effect their ritual in the waters they once rowed while alive.

Take Interstate Route 95 to Interstate Route 195 East. Take Route 114 South over the Mount Hope Bridge. Bear left onto Route 24 into Tiverton. Take Route 77 along the shore to Nanaquaket Road. The sightings are in this area and happen mostly during the evening.

SIN AND FLESH BROOK

Fort Barton in Tiverton, Rhode Island, offers a 2.3-mile loop where hikers can explore an important parcel of history and take in some of the most stunning views the state has to offer. The trail is not hard to navigate, being mostly flat, and if you hear gunfire, do not be alarmed. What you're hearing is not a ghostly battle being replayed but the noise from a nearby firing range. If some Indigenous people attack a person dressed in minister's clothing, that is not a reenactment. You have just witnessed the ghosts of Sin and Flesh Brook reliving the moment that gave the waterway its rather macabre name. Sin and Flesh Brook runs southwest from the area near Fish Road and Route 24, terminating at Nanaquaket (also spelled Nannaquaket) Pond. The best way to see it—and, perhaps, the ghosts—is hiking on the Fort Barton Woods trails.

On March 28, 1676, Quaker minister Zoeth Howland mounted his steed and left his Dartmouth, Massachusetts home to travel to Newport, Rhode Island, for a meeting. Traveling alone during this period was dangerous due to the raiding Native parties roaming the woods in small bands. Howland felt the Lord would protect him as he and his steed meandered along the small trail that would take him to his destination. He had covered fifteen miles of the thirty-mile trip when he, tragically, became a casualty of the war. As he reached the path in Tiverton, six hostile Indians ambushed him. The Quaker preacher was tortured and killed. His mutilated body was found in an unnamed stream still running red with his lifeblood. The stream became

Sin and Flesh Brook in Tiverton, Rhode Island, which Zoeth Howland haunts to this day. *Photo courtesy of Arlene Nicholson.*

known as Sinning Flesh River in remembrance of the horrific event. Over the years, the name evolved to Sin and Flesh Brook.

People may now travel the paths along the river and the fort without fear of danger, but Zoeth, still trying to get to his meeting, makes his way among the leaves and bushes along the banks of the watercourse. People claim to have heard ethereal screams from the direction of the river and have even seen the river run red with blood. Zoeth has appeared before more than one hiker on the trail that still traverses the area where he was killed. The ghastly event has played itself out, sometimes in front of astonished witnesses and perhaps other times when no one is there to witness it, just as there was no one when Howland met his fate. The trail loop is worth a visit, whether you are looking for scenery or paranormal activity. Thanks to six Indians and a Quaker minister, Fort Barton is one of the places that harbors ghosts from King Philip's War.

Sin and Flesh Brook is located on the eastern side of Tiverton. Follow the directions above to the Sakonnet River. Just past Nanaquaket Road will be Bridgeport Road. Take a left onto Bridgeport Road and then a right onto Old Main Road. The brook crosses under the road at its starting point where the little pond on the right is. The trail leads to Fort Barton, the ruins of a small Revolutionary War fort, as it snakes back and forth over the river.

NINE MEN'S MISERY

Perhaps the most tragic battle the English endured during the war was what is now termed Pierce's Fight. Captain Michael Pierce led a group of approximately sixty Plymouth Colony militia and twenty converted Wampanoag Indians in pursuit of Narragansetts led by Conanchet, who, during the conflict, burned several Rhode Island settlements, including Warwick and Providence (burned on March 29, 1676), and attacked Plymouth. Intelligence reports concluded they were going to Attleborough to raid that settlement. It was Pierce's company that was sent to intercept the raiders.

On Sunday, March 26, 1676, Pierce's men came across some of Conanchet's men lingering in the woods as if lame or wounded. Pierce, a brave and stout fighter, decided to follow them. As they reached the banks of the Blackstone River in what is now Central Falls, Pierce realized he and his company had walked into an ambush. Conanchet's warriors came from everywhere, outnumbering Pierce's men almost eight to one. The militia circled and defended themselves as best they could. Pierce fell early in the fight. A Christian Indian named Amos stood by Pierce's side, and as Amos later recalled, when Pierce was injured, Amos fired on the enemy until he saw there was no possibility for him to do any good to Captain Pierce and his men.

Nearly all were killed, including Captain Pierce and most of the Wampanoags. The Narragansetts lost only a handful of warriors. Those who were able to escape used desperate means. Some of the converts saw that the enemy had blackened their faces and followed suit. One saved a fellow militiaman by pretending to chase him into the woods with a hatchet until they were safely away. Amos blackened his face with ash and proceeded to mingle with the enemy until he was able to hide among the bushes and escape. His actions helped historians better piece together the events of the massacre, as he was one of the few to be able to relate, at least in his own words, what happened that day. Those who escaped fled to wherever they were safe. Ten men, however, were captured and marched three miles to a spot in what is now Cumberland, Rhode Island, where they were dispatched after being tortured. Out of the ten, one man survived the ordeal. This place became known as Nine Men's Misery.

Earlier that morning, Pierce had dispatched a messenger to Captain Edmunds of Providence with a request for backup in the pending attack. The messenger felt obligated to attend morning service before delivering his

Nine Men's Misery monument deep in the woods of the Cumberland Monastery. *Photo courtesy of Arlene Nicholson.*

communication. Edmunds immediately chastised him for his tardiness in delivering such an important request, although it has been widely accepted that Edmunds's men would have done little good in saving Pierce due to the number of enemy attackers that day.

The Reverend Noah Newman of Rehoboth sent a letter containing the names of those killed in battle. Among them were fifty-five English and eleven Praying Indians. The paper became worn and mutilated so that several names were lost. Of the nine slain at Nine Men's Misery, research has uncovered four names: John Low, John Miller Jr., John Fitz Jr. and Benjamin Bucklin. In *The Soldiers of King Philip's War*, George Bodge wrote,

> *The paper is much worn and mutilated, so that the names of several are lost. It is said that Miller and Fitz were of Rehoboth, and probably others. Seven or eight names are needed, in addition, to make up the fifty-five.*

Contrary to some claims, the men were not beheaded, and their heads were not placed on poles. The Bucklin Society recorded:

> *When the nine were found, they were buried in the same spot they perished, somewhere near the monument. In 1790, a Dr. Bowen of Providence*

began to disinter the remains in search for one man, Benjamin Bucklin. It was known that this Rehoboth Militiaman was of extraordinary size and had a double set of teeth. One of the skeletons dug up was of extraordinary size, and by the fact of its having a double set of teeth, was recognized as that of Benjamin Bucklin [Buckland]*, of Rehoboth. It is assured thus that the men were from other colonies than that of Providence.*

The locals found out about and interrupted the disinterment, but not before the doctor had found what he was looking for. The names of the others who were killed to this day remain a mystery.

In 1928, the remains of the nine men were dug up and transported in a crate to be stored by the Rhode Island Historical Society. It appeared that the Trappist monks who owned the land at the time objected to having an unconsecrated burial on their property. The crate stayed with the society, unopened, until 1976, when the remains were reinterred at their present location on the three hundredth anniversary of the fight and the two hundredth anniversary of U.S. independence.

The area of Nine Men's Misery is one of the major hot spots for haunts from King Philip's War. Screams are sometimes heard echoing through the woods around the monument—horrific screams that resemble those of someone in mortal agony. The ghost of a small child appears near the swamp just to the left of the monument. Rumors hold that she drowned in the swamp either by accident or during the conflict when she came upon the marauders and their captives. The remains of a home and other farm structures are nearby. She may have been one of the family members who lived on the property, yet no modern record of any child drowning in the swamp has been uncovered to date.

A ghostly rider suddenly appears on the trail, stopping with his spectral horse kicking up and snorting before turning and galloping off into the void. The sound of galloping and a horse whinnying presages the appearance of the phantom rider. The trails are easily discerned for some distance, and the woods are sparse enough that a horse and rider could not find camouflage from curious eyes without great difficulty. One person was at the monument when she heard muffled screams that sounded more like the deadly massacre was being replayed centuries after it had originally taken place. Visitors often feel a strong tension in the air, as it suddenly gets very heavy. People visiting the monument and surrounding area sometimes feel like there are eyes behind every tree and rock, spying on them. Many get this sudden feeling of dread just before faint, frantic cries and screams permeate the air along the trails as if the woods are reliving some of the battles where so many were lost. It is believed to be the oldest war monument in the nation, and although the men are buried near and around the marker, it still gives off a foreboding sense of dread when one realizes the reason why the monument was erected in the first place.

If you decide to hike out to the monument, start at the trail just over the guardrail and stay to the right, then follow the red markers. While you are there, you may want to check out the library, as it also haunted. The building was once home to a Cistercian monastery, and the ghost of a monk still wanders the halls upstairs and in the rear of the building.

SQUAW HOLLOW AND ROCK CAVE

If you should find yourself on Route 140 in East Freetown, Massachusetts, you may want to keep your eyes peeled while passing through Squaw Hollow. For generations, travelers have reported seeing an Indigenous woman sitting by the side of the road weaving a piece of fabric. The legend of this ghost has been passed down for centuries. Some believe she is a relic of King Philip's War or, perhaps, from a time way before the war broke out. The most startling aspect of this haunting is the fact that her head is in her lap as she goes about her ethereal chore of eternally weaving her spectral cloth.

A little farther down Route 140 is a place called Rock Cave or Rocky Woods. Here, hikers come upon a rock formation that forms a natural cave. King Philip allegedly spent the last night of his mortal life in this cave. It is there that he had the most ominous dream of being slain by the enemy in his own home. The dream was fulfilled the next day when he returned to his headquarters and home at Mount Hope in Bristol, Rhode Island. Voices speaking in Native American tongues are sometimes heard around the cave, and some who have hiked the trail reported the feeling of being watched by unfriendly presences. Freetown was part of the most concentrated area of fighting and brutality during the war. It is no wonder there are strong remnants still lingering.

ASSONET LEDGE AND THE PHANTOM FIRES

Within the Freetown/Fall River State Forest (commonly shortened to Freetown Forest), many strange occurrences related to King Philip's War and the Wampanoag people that once called the area home can be witnessed. The forest covers over 5,000 acres within the city of Fall River, the town of Lakeville and one-third of Freetown. The publicly owned preserve has over fifty miles of unpaved roads and trails. The forest is also home to a 227-acre Wampanoag reservation. Author and historian Christopher Balzano has written extensively on the area called the Bridgewater Triangle and the Freetown/Fall River State Forest, which lies within the triangle.

Balzano has always been amused when someone uses the term "ancient Indian burial ground." When someone begins a ghost story with "There was this ancient Indian burial ground," eyebrows raise and interest is suddenly piqued. The listener is compelled to ask, "What happened because of this ancient burial ground?" "Is it sacred?" "Is it cursed?" "Did the ancient spirits rise from their tombs and exact revenge on the White settlers for encroaching on their sacred resting place?"

In fact, almost all the Native burial grounds in New England are ancient, or at least very old. Archaeological digs in certain areas around the region have uncovered Native burial grounds dating back thousands of years. And yes, like the burying yards and cemeteries of those who came after, they are considered sacred. The Freetown/Fall River State Forest reportedly contains a fair share of these ancient burial grounds, but many, due to the ravages of time and nature, are now lost to the human eye.

What can be seen on occasion in different areas of the woods are what witnesses call phantom fires. When the perceiver of the phenomenon investigates, they find that the fires give off no sound, smoke or heat. The glow of the fire is contained to a small area above the ghostly flame. As soon as they appear, they vanish, leaving no trace of a blaze in the spot. In some cases, the woods are so thick or difficult to navigate that it would be improbable or senseless to set up a camp in the particular spot where the fire is seen.

Many believe the phantom fires are a residual haunt, a moment in time recorded long ago and replaying when the conditions are right. The fires are replays of the past when Indigenous people camped on the land. They tend to appear randomly within the forest, giving the illusion that someone or something has set up camp for the night.

One of the most haunted places within the Freetown/Fall River State Forest is a rocky outcropping called Assonet Ledge. The cliff one sees today was mostly formed by the Fall River Granite Company in the 1800s. For years, local youths have used it as a gathering place for parties. Not so for the Wampanoags, who shunned it due to the negative energy surrounding the precipice. It is not recorded how much of a ledge or rocky outcropping existed before the company began quarrying, but there had to have been some sort of cliff for them to discover and commence digging the granite from the earth. The presence of an existing ledge of some sort gives credence to the Wampanoags relating the fear of a ledge before the company began taking the granite from the area.

Shadow people are often seen in the surrounding forest. Reports of hideous-looking creatures flitting among the trees and brush have scared many a visitor to the preserve. Some people who climb to the top of the Assonet Ledge report a very heavy feeling of sadness suddenly overcoming them. The feeling becomes so intense that they are compelled to leap off the edge to their possible demise.

Several people have died from falling over the ledge or have drowned in the waters below. Some who have taken the plunge claim they were pushed by an unseen force—which may be a mystical creature called a Pukwudgie, known to entrance people to the top of the cliff before pushing them over. Pukwudgies are small creatures of Indian lore. They can appear and disappear at will. They reside predominantly within the area called the Bridgewater Triangle, where they remain mostly unseen. Many people in the region of the triangle, either residing there or visiting, have witnessed the small Pukwudgies roaming about. They are said to be very dangerous. When seen, do not approach or attempt to communicate with them, as they will surely lure you to your death.

One of the main theories about why the ledge may hold such negativity dates to King Philip's War. Many of the Natives, knowing that capture by the English meant torture, dishonorable death or being sold into slavery, chose to climb to the top of the ledge and jump off rather than face the indignity of surrender.

To this day, visitors roaming the area of the ledge hear what sounds like war whoops and see the ghosts of warriors moving about the trees and rocks of the ledge. The area where the state forest sits is obviously magical, whether it be positive or negative energies permeating the land. Legends, haunts and strange tales abound in the forest. It is obvious the Natives were aware of the unworldly powers the woods held—and still do.

The mysterious and haunted Assonet Ledge in Freetown State Forest. *Photo courtesy of Peter Muise and http://newenglandfolklore.blogspot.com.*

Getting there is half the fun, and you never know what you will see once inside the forest. Take Route 24 to the Freetown exit, then look for Copicut Road. Take a left and follow this road to the intersection of Bell Rock Road. The Wampanoag Reservation sign will be on your right. Take a right down Bell Rock Road. Shortly, you will see a state forest entrance on your right.

Once inside the entrance, you will see the Indian meetinghouse, and the dirt road, Ledge Road, continues. You may hike or drive to the ledge if the road is not filled with ruts. The hike is only about one and a half hours round trip.

Near the end of Ledge Road, there are two street signs: Ledge Road and Upper Ledge Road. Upper Ledge Road offers an old Civilian Conservation Corps stone bridge and a large, mossy water hole; you will do all the climbing gradually, by road, and finish on the top of the ledge. Ledge Road will take you through some pine groves and end up at the base of the ledge.

PROFILE ROCK

Many people come to the Freetown/Fall River State Forest to visit an uncanny formation called Profile Rock. Although the fifty-foot-high natural wonder sits just outside the preserve, it is still considered part of the state forest. The rock, once considered the Massachusetts version of New Hampshire's Old Man of the Mountain, was said to resemble the profile of Massasoit, the great Indian chief who made the original fifty-year peace treaty with the Pilgrims. It was once known as a meeting place for the Wampanoags because its features resembled one of their kind. Spirits are said to linger there to this day, chiefly that of Massasoit's son, King Philip.

Philip often came to the profile to meditate and contemplate the affairs between his people and the English. It was also where Philip held secret meetings with his generals and warriors during the war. In the waning days of the war, Philip is said to have climbed the stone edifice and solemnly looked out on the land he once ruled and knew he was about to lose. His spirit, being sadly broken at that moment, left a portion of itself behind to haunt forever the very place where he once sought wisdom and advice.

Visitors to the rock claim to have seen the ghost of a dark-skinned man standing on top of the formation, making gestures as if performing some sort of ceremonial prayer or ritual. Some have seen the figure sitting atop the profile, staring sadly out over the land. Either way, the figure vanishes into thin air within a few moments. Strange lights like glowing green and white orbs are often seen floating about the area around the rock. According to Native legend, "ghost dancers" performed ceremonial dances around the rock to conjure the spirits of their ancestors. This is also where Philip allegedly gave his prized wampum belt to his second-in-command, Annawan.

Unfortunately, on June 19, 2019, at approximately 9:22 a.m., the Freetown Police and Fire Departments were called to the forest for a report of damage to the historic rock formation. The first responders and park officials discovered that a large portion of the rock formation had broken off and fallen to pieces below. Time had finally caused the great boulder, thought by so many to resemble Massasoit, to give up the ghost. The real ghosts continue to roam among the rubble and rock that is mostly a memory to some yet still an eternal home to others.

Profile Rock is located on what is called Joshua Mountain, named after Joshua Tisdale, the first White settler near the site. Former Freetown

An old image of Profile Rock in the Freetown State Forest. *Public domain, from authors' collection.*

selectman Ben Evans owned it for several years before selling it to the state to be used as a tourist attraction. Profile Rock sits at the park's northern end and is easily reached from the parking area. It is about a ten-minute walk, roughly half a mile from the road to the rock.

WILLIE WOODHEAD TRAIL

Glocester, Rhode Island, is a sparsely settled rural town with many legends of gold, pirates (yes, pirates), monsters and haunted places. In the western section of the town, on the Connecticut border, lies a parcel of land called Durfee Hill Management Area. Within this preserve, one will find a place called Dark Swamp where a creature named the Glocester Ghoul is said to lurk.

The legend of the monster was little known until horror/science fiction writer Howard Phillips Lovecraft and his friend fellow horror writer Clifford Martin Eddy went in search of the creature Lovecraft referred to in his writings as IT. On September 19 and August 4, 1923, Lovecraft took the trolley to Chepachet, a hamlet of Glocester, before traversing Route 44 to the Dark Swamp area.

The creature's legend dates to the colonists' first settling in the region. The Indigenous people were thought to have laid a curse on the land to keep the colonists from encroaching on their hunting and camping grounds. Old-timers said that several of the first White settlers who did not heed the Natives' warnings entered the swamp and were never seen again.

Lovecraft and Eddy may not have found the creature on that hot day in August, but in their travels through the wooded area, they surely must have passed by something that neither paid too much heed to—something that, if they knew what it was, would have spun an amazing and haunting tale about them.

Just past the Dark Swamp, strewn about the woods and along the trail, are great piles of rocks referred to as cairns. According to old-timers, these man-made formations were the burial mounds of Native warriors who fell during a little-recorded skirmish during King Philip's War. Some have brought forth the idea that this may have actually been one of the Nipsachuck battles but was erroneously given credit for taking place in the area of North Smithfield that it is now named for.

The stone mounds measure several feet in length and range from four to six feet in height. There are about thirty-five of them scattered about the woods within eye shot of the trail. When Native warriors fell during battle, instead of being buried, it was considered more honorable to cover them with stone mounds where they fell. Where the trail runs between the mounds, the area takes on a more ethereal tone, as if someone is watching those who hike past the stone piles.

Much of the trail and other parts of the woods near Elbow Rock Road follow the alignment of an old Native American trail. The preserve was obviously very important to the early people of the land, so much so that they created a horrible creature to protect it from the colonists' encroachment. The mounds may also be protected by the great spirits that escorted the fallen warriors to their glory in the sky. A walk through the trails is well worth the adventure; just beware of the swamp, the ghoul and, perhaps, the spirits of those who may rest eternally in repose under the great cairns.

From Route 94 in West Glocester, take Old Snake Hill Road east. Turn left onto George Allen Road, then take a sharp right onto Willie Woodhead Road. Park on the left of the cul-de-sac and continue on foot until you reach a sandy circle off to the left. Cross the circle and stay to the left. Head downhill, and you will see Dark Swamp. The trails can be misleading, so a map of the area is most helpful. One trail will lead you past Dark Swamp and another small swamp. This leads to the remnants of a farm and, eventually, the cairns.

QUEEN'S FORT

One of the most historically significant sites that remains from King Philip's War is a place in Exeter, Rhode Island, called Queen's Fort. The stone structure served as a refuge for Quaiapen, the Indigenous female sachem who rallied survivors of the Great Swamp fight along with other tribes along the Connecticut/Rhode Island border. The site, only a few miles from an English fort, was not discovered until after the war.

Queen Quaiapen, also known as Queen Magnus, Maquas, Maquus or Matantuck, was the sister of the chief sachem of the Niantics, Ninigret, and wife of Mriksah, eldest son of the great Narragansett sachem Conanicus. In 1676, the elderly queen, with about two hundred warriors, women and children, took refuge at this site built by an Indian named Stonewall John. John had learned the art of masonry from the English, and his skills became of great use to the Indians when the conflict broke out.

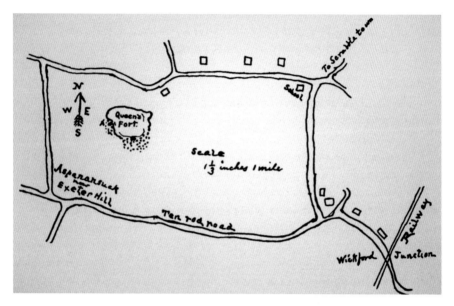

An illustration of the location of Queen's Fort in Exeter. *Public domain, from authors' collection.*

Here in this well-secluded place, Queen Quaiapen and her people held out, until she was finally persuaded to move north to a swamp in what is now North Smithfield, Rhode Island.

J.R. Cole writes in his book *History of Washington and Kent Counties*:

> *Queen's Fort is a celebrated place and affords historical features. It is situated in the northeastern portion of the town, and is a curiously shaped hill, somewhat like a half globe. The sides of this hill on the east, southeast and south are covered with a mass of stones more or less irregular in shape, and so thrown together as to form natural caverns and retreats.…On the top of the hill is a stone wall fortifying its approach. The wall runs east and west, and at either corner were once stone huts, probably the residence of some Indian chief. From both of these points the wall runs south, but only for a short distance, the south side being naturally fortified. William Reynolds resided here some forty or fifty years ago. In a small valley just west of the wall is a unique collection of stones forming a natural cavern, in which it is said Maquus, the squaw sachem, once resided, but the chamber is now nearly filled with rubbish. A little to the west of this once enticing retreat for the savage heroine is a sand bank where the soldiers on their celebrated march from Richard Smith's house toward the big swamp halted, expecting to find a body of Indians whom they intended to attack. But upon reaching*

this place the soldiers found that the Indians had returned to their fortress, leaving them only a quantity of corn which was secured.

The fort has been compromised over the years by the ravages of time, vandalism and the taking of the stones for one reason or another. Very old drawings and photos show what it looked like many years, even centuries, ago. According to Sidney Rider in his book *The Lands of Rhode Island as They Were Known to Caunounicus and Miantunnomu*, the fort is the last ancient structure in existence built by the Narragansetts.

The fort was roughly square, with three walls stretching two hundred feet into the woods and one massive wall made impenetrable by a massive pile of boulders. According to old drawings and maps, it was quite a formidable site. It also harbors some ethereal presences, as people have heard what appear to be voices flitting about the ruins on occasion. These may be the residuals of the band that took sanctuary among the rocks. Many lost families and all they had during the brutal Great Swamp fight. Their melancholy phantom

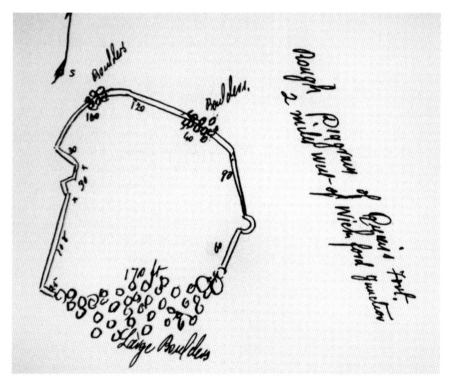

Rough diagram of the construction of Queen's Fort in Exeter. *Public domain, from authors' collection.*

verbalization is unintelligible, yet it continues centuries after many used this as the last safe haven they would ever know. The queen and her followers were all but wiped out during the second battle of Nipsachuck on July 2, 1676. Perhaps many have returned in spirit to seek eternal refuge in the place that, for a short time during the war, gave them peace.

NIPSACHUCK

Descendants of the Narragansetts have long maintained that the area known as Nipsachuck on the Smithfield and North Smithfield line was a ceremonial and camping place for their people dating back centuries before the arrival of Europeans. Around 2006, the site was rediscovered when a development company sought to build a 122-lot subdivision on the property. Artifacts and burial cairns were found, and all work halted, prompting an archaeological dig to uncover the depth of the history. The site was found to be a few thousand years old.

The area was also the focus of two battles during King Philip's War. The first battle was not as monumental as the second one, which took place on July 2, 1676—one of the last battles of King Philip's War to be fought in southern New England. Military historians and scholars find it most interesting because it included the first-time use of a cavalry charge on horseback by the English colonists.

During the summer of 1676, Quaiapen and over one hundred of her followers, mainly women and children, sought refuge from the hostilities of King Philip's War near Nipsachuck Swamp. On July 2, they were attacked by Major John Talcott and his cavalry force. The actual skirmish took place at Mattity Swamp along Mattity Road. The Narragansetts fled into the swamp, where many were killed, including Quaiapen. This conflict spelled the end of organized Narragansett opposition in the war. Quaiapen was a powerful Niantic female sachem through birth and marriage and was the last Narragansett-Niantic leader to be captured or killed in King Philip's War (1675–76).

Excavations conducted at Nipsachuck through the National Park Service American Battlefield Protection Program uncovered 150 battle-related and domestic objects within a sixty-seven-acre parcel. Battle-related objects included musket balls, flintlock flints, brass arrow points, horseshoes, shoeing nails, a bridle rosette, firearms and firearm parts. Other artifacts included a

Mattity Swamp in North Smithfield, Rhode Island, where Queen Quaiapen drowned while attempting to escape the English. *Photo courtesy of Arlene Nicholson.*

Another swamp in the Nipsachuck area where Queen Quaiapen's warriors attempted to escape the English forces. *Photo courtesy of Arlene Nicholson.*

One of several caves at the edge of Nipsachuck where Quaiapen's people hid from the English. *Photo courtesy of Arlene Nicholson.*

A development now sits on part of the site where the battle of Nipsachuck took place. *Photo courtesy of Arlene Nicholson.*

bell, a brass pendant, a carved quahog fragment, pewter buttons and a piece of a jaw harp.

With so many remnants of battle, it is no surprise that remnants of the people who fought there that day are also still lingering. Paranormal investigator Charles Gardner performed an investigation at the site and recorded what sounded like a woman in distress. The area of the swamp is just a small part of what is called Nipsachuck. During the brutal conflict, many retreated to other areas, running for a few miles. Some hid in rocky outcroppings, while others attempted to forge through the swamps. Nipsachuck has its share of both. Unfortunately, the swamps would prove a poor choice.

As for the ghosts, there are plenty of stories of ethereal Natives seen wandering among the ledges or darting through the woods. Strange cries are heard from the swamps and deep in the woods. As this was a sacred site for the tribes that wandered the area, it would be natural to assume there are spirits watching over their former camp. Unfortunately, most of the land Nipsachuck occupies is private property, but there are some places along the side of the road where one may stop and take in a little history or perhaps witness some long-ago moment that took place during the battles.

SQUAW ROCK

Squaw Rock, located in Plainfield, Connecticut, is part of a preserve called Squaw Rock State Park. The rock is a conglomeration of boulders that fell from the cliffs above. The jagged three-hundred-foot granite embankment looms over one hundred feet above the deep gorge that was once a portion of it. The falling of the boulders created many caves and caverns, which can be explored while visiting the site.

One of the most interesting of the caves is called Squaw's Kitchen. The cave interior is roughly twelve by twelve feet and has a cleft in the rocks, forming a natural chimney. It is placed in such a way that when ice forms in the chimney, it remains throughout most of the summer.

Local tribes often held councils at the rock and used the caves as meeting rooms or perhaps even sweat lodges. During King Philip's War and for some time after, various tribal members found refuge in the caves. Women and children hid out in the caves for fear of being captured, killed or sold into slavery by the English. After the war, some made it their permanent residence, knowing the seclusion would keep them from English eyes. Slowly, those who called the caverns home died off until one lonely woman remained. She tended to her business day in and day out, cooking in the natural kitchen and sleeping in another part of the caves until she finally went to her creator.

The area became a popular picnic spot for families, who began to give the caves and other features of the formation names like Devil's Kitchen, Old Lady's Stove, the Dancing Floor, Fiddler's Stand and Pulpit Rock. There are many caves to explore: one is about forty feet long, while others are shorter but tall enough to venture into. Mike Girard of the Strange New England website describes the caves in much detail, including the Old Lady's Kitchen, which has two chambers along with a natural chimney that was "still blackened from the soot of the fire[s] from long ago" and the remnants of a stone fire ring. Ellen Larned wrote about the caves in her book on the history of Windham County, describing their popularity with the people who knew of their existence.

Visitors to the site to this day stand in awe of the many caves and characteristics of Squaw Rock. They may also encounter some of the past residents who once called the caves home. People visiting the area have witnessed smoke coming from the kitchen's chimney, but when they investigate, there is no one there and no fire. Some have seen shadows moving about the rock and the entrances of the caves. Whether they are shadows of wildlife or the ghosts of those who once called the rock home is a matter of conjecture.

THE GHOST OF JOHN GALLUP

Captain John Gallup was born in Dorsetshire, England, on January 25, 1620. After his family moved to the colonies, John Jr. grew up at what is now called Whitehall Mansion in Mystic, Connecticut. While a young boy, along with his father and brothers, he became involved with the Pequot Wars, during which the English aided the Narragansetts in ridding the area of the Pequots. During this conflict, a friend and fellow soldier went searching for a sailing vessel stolen by the Pequots. He gave orders to come looking for him if he did not return within an allotted time. When John and his father discovered the vessel near Block Island, they rammed it with their ship, taking the stolen boat back into their possession. They also discovered,

The grave of Captain John Gallup of Mystic, Connecticut, on the property of Smith's Castle. *Photo courtesy of Arlene Nicholson.*

aboard the boat, the head of their friend. From that day on, John Jr. was lifelong enemy of the Natives.

John Jr. married Hannah Lake in 1643 in Boston, Massachusetts, and later moved to Stonington, Connecticut, where he owned a vast piece of land along the Mystic River. He became well known in local politics as well as the militia. In January 1675, he was made captain of the First Company of the Connecticut Regiment. When King Philip's War broke out, he was very active in several of the skirmishes, one of which would prove fatal.

On December 19, 1675, Captain Gallup helped lead the charge in the Great Swamp Fight. His valiance in the charge was short-lived; a musket ball to the head killed him instantly. Ten men of his company also died with him that day. He was among the soldiers buried at Smith's Blockhouse, now Smith's Castle in North Kingstown, Rhode Island. A memorial was put in place at the family plot in Whitehall Burial Ground, Mystic, Connecticut, in 1969, where the remains of his wife and other family members lie in eternal repose.

The dust of Captain Gallup's mortal frame may lie buried in North Kingstown, but his ghost is quite active in the family burial lot in Mystic. Courtney McInvale runs Seaside Shadows Haunted History Tours, and one of the places the tour visits is the burial yard. According to witnesses, Captain Gallup's ghost has been seen standing atop his monument in full uniform with his sword drawn and held high. During two of the tours, a man was seen walking toward the memorial, but when someone went to check, no one was there. The graveyard is closed to other visitors during the tour, so it was highly unlikely someone would have been in the grounds at that time. The sound of footsteps marching around the stone has also been heard during the tours.

Courtney once recorded a disembodied voice at the monument that simply said, "William." William was not only John's brother but also the name of John's son. It was William, Captain Gallup's son, who later became great friends with the Pequots—so much so that he would have them over for suppers and major events such as weddings and the like.

Many believe this may be the reason Captain Gallup haunts the family cemetery and not where he was actually buried. His aversion toward the Indigenous peoples and the fact that he was killed by one was well known. His son befriending the enemy, in his mind, may very well be why he shows up in uniform at his memorial.

The Whitehall Mansion one sees today was built on the foundation of the Gallup home around 1771 by Dr. Dudley Woodbridge. The original home may have been dismantled and the timbers used in the building of the newer one. In 1962, the mansion was moved to make room for highway expansion before being given to the Stonington Historical Society. The building was given a new foundation as well, but the rest of the structure remained as it was when first erected.

The building was added to the National Register of Historic Places on April 12, 1979. The mansion remained in the care of the Stonington Historical Society until 1996. Purchased and renovated, the Whitehall Mansion opened its doors to the public to become the premier historical inn of Mystic, Connecticut. It is also one of the more haunted places in that area.

Some spirits call the attic of the inn their home. From 1862 to 1872, the Wheeler family reportedly hid runaway slaves there as part of the Underground Railroad. Betsy's Room contains the stairwell leading to the attic. A strange feeling of dread and a sense of being watched sometimes permeate the room. Footsteps and muffled voices are heard from the empty attic.

Children giggling and laughing while running past Lucy's Room are often heard. This is rather strange, because children are not allowed at the inn due to the many precious and delicate antiques displayed about the rooms. Items tend to move on their own, vanishing from one place and appearing in another. Misty forms are seen moving about on occasion.

One of the main ghosts of the inn is Lucy Woodbridge, Dr. Woodbridge's daughter. She is seen wandering about at all times of the day and night. Book a night or two at the inn and take in Seaside Shadows' Haunted History Tours, the Downtown Mystic Tour or the Mystic Moonlit Graveyard Ghost Tour. For more info, visit https://www.seasideshadows.com.

THE GREEN, NORTH CARVER, MASSACHUSETTS

Although no longer there, the Green in North Carver, Massachusetts, was the site of King Philip's Spring. The green was called Lakenham Green before having its named changed, but history still reverberates around the small triangle that became a gruesome part of the war. Not many know that there was once a spring running from the green. When Philip's warriors attacked what is now Chiltonville, a small hamlet of Plymouth, it was a calculated move. The home of William Clark sat along the bank of the Eel River. Clark was the most prominent merchant in Plymouth at the time, trading also with the Natives in the area. In fact, one day before the raid, a warrior by the name of Keweenam had visited Clark's home, scouting out the goods and necessities along with the best areas for entry and egress. The home was also a store for military commodities, making it a major target for the enemy to plunder.

The attack on the home was planned for Sunday, as the Natives knew the families would be at the meetinghouse and the home would be vacant. On March 12, 1676, eleven Indians raided the home but were surprised to see two families still there. According to records, Mrs. Clark and her infant were killed, their eight-year-old son was "knocked on the head" but survived and all the others were slaughtered. Eleven in all lost their lives that morning, and the home was set ablaze. On returning from the attack, the warriors stopped at the spring to wash the blood of the victims from their hands and bodies.

The spring was filled in long ago, but the place still radiates with energy as the blood of innocent lives ran into the soil, forever staining it. Some people feel sorrow or a heavy sense of something negative when standing where the spring once bubbled. Empaths say they can feel the terror of the victims' plight from the blood that sank into the soil and scarred it so many years ago.

REDEMPTION ROCK

On February 10, 1676, several hundred Native warriors under the guidance of King Philip raided Lancaster, Massachusetts, destroying the village. The garrison house of the Reverend Joseph Rowlandson, the first minister of that town, was attacked; seventeen of its inhabitants were massacred, and twenty-four men, women and children were taken prisoner, forced to live in the wild for several months. Those who survived their captivity were later redeemed (a popular term used at the time for being traded or ransomed for something in exchange). Among them was the preacher's wife, Mary, and their three children. For eleven weeks, the captives were marched from camp to camp, living with the warriors and experiencing firsthand the tactics of their enemy.

Sign for the site of Redemption Rock on Route 140 in Princeton, Massachusetts, where Mary Rowlandson was traded back to the English for supplies. *Photo courtesy of Arlene Nicholson.*

Grave marker of six-year-old Sarah Rowlandson, daughter of Mary Rowlandson, who died in captivity in 1676. *Photo courtesy of Arlene Nicholson.*

In late April 1676, thanks to the pleas of the Reverend John Hoar of Concord, Massachusetts, Mary was ransomed back to the English for cloth, provisions and money. Hoar was a minister, military leader and trusted Indian liaison during the war. He is buried in the Old Hill Burial Ground in Concord, Massachusetts. On May 2, 1676, the parties met on a great boulder, where the trade was made. This became a monumental event due to the fact that Mary would later write her account of events in one of the most important books ever published about the conflict. Her narrative of her captivity, called in full *The Sovereignty and Goodness of God: Being a Narrative of the Captivity and Restoration of Mrs. Mary Rowlandson*, was published in Cambridge in 1682. It remains as a vital window into the times and is considered a flagship example of the American literary genre of captivity narratives.

Mary's two surviving children would later be redeemed, joining her and her husband in Boston. Unfortunately, Sarah, the youngest, died in captivity on February 18 after suffering a gunshot wound during the raid. She died in the Wenimessit Indian camp near Lancaster, and a memorial marker was placed in front of a cemetery on Hardwick Road in New Braintree.

The rock and a quarter acre of surrounding land were acquired by the Trustees of Reservations in 1953 and are open to the public. An inscription carved in the rock reads,

> *Upon this rock May 2, 1676, was made the agreement for the ransom of Mrs. Mary Rowlandson of Lancaster between the Indians and John Hoar of Concord. King Philip was with the Indians but refused to consent.*

Visitors to the site not only relish the history but sometimes see it replaying as well. Although many get an overwhelming sensation of the past, some have witnessed what appears to be a ghostly reenactment of the trade that took place over three centuries ago. The specters of Indians and colonists appear on the rock as if waiting for someone or discussing business. The energy there is powerful, to say the least. Some have claimed the area is packed with ghosts of the colonists, roaming the small parcel of land and its outer vicinity. It appears the monumental moment in time had enough impact to imprint itself on the land to be replayed over and over. Redemption Rock may be part of our past, but it seems the past keeps coming back, perhaps to remind us never to repeat it.

Redemption Rock in Princeton, Massachusetts. *Photo courtesy of Arlene Nicholson.*

This inscription on Redemption Rock tells of the trade with Philip's men for the release of Mary Rowlandson. *Photo courtesy of Arlene Nicholson.*

Redemption Rock is located on Route 140 in Princeton, Massachusetts. There is a sign on Route 140 where a parking lot sits next to the historic boulder with its inscription.

NIPMUCK FISHING FIRES

From generation to generation, a legend has been handed down about an event that forever blemished the land and, mostly, the waters in the northeastern section of Connecticut. Much like in the story of Lake Alexander (see the upcoming section on Lake Alexander), the Great Spirit avenged those who had wronged the moral fiber of the Indigenous holy one.

The Nipmucks inhabited most of the northeastern portion of Connecticut and a good part of central Massachusetts. Their name basically means "freshwater people." They fished the waters, which were abundant in aquatic catch, especially the sweet-tasting eels they had become most fond of. Such luck in their ability to have an endless supply of food was credited to the Great Spirit, who, they concluded, had seen great favor in them, therefore blessing the waters with ever-flowing bounty.

One day, a group of Nipmuck campers came upon a band of Narragansett hunters. The Narragansetts were their neighbors to the south, who, like them, also fished the waters of their respective territory. The Narragansetts had fresh and salt water to fish in, so they were no strangers to the food the Nipmucks enjoyed. The Nipmuck band, having just caught a large supply of eel, offered to share some with the Narragansett hunters. During the repast, a few of the Narragansetts began bragging about how their preparation of eel was far tastier than the bland recipes their hosts had offered. They commented on how ill flavored and poorly cooked the eel had been and how they would rather not have any more.

Predictably, harsh words flew back and forth until a full-fledged fight ensued. The Nipmucks, being much greater in numbers, killed all but two of the Narragansetts, who escaped back to their neck of the woods, informing their tribesmen of the massacre. This angered the heads of the Narragansetts, for the laws of hospitality were very sacred to the Indigenous people. Even the most hated enemy, when invited into a camp, would be treated with the utmost respect and generosity. The Nipmucks had broken one of the most sacred laws of the Great Spirit. The Narragansetts did not have to worry about retaliation, for they knew the Great Spirit would deal with this atrocity in his own way.

That very night, strange yellow and blue lights began to rise from the waters, streaking across the sky and hovering over the Nipmuck tribe. They were struck with sheer terror, for they knew the lights were the spirits of the slain Narragansetts returning to seek revenge. The tribe's people began to beg for forgiveness, chanting and weeping in hopes of repentance. They banged their drums and danced all night, begging the Great Spirit for his mercy. Apparently, the Great Spirit never forgave them. Every time the ghostly lights appeared in the swamps and outlying edges of the lakes and ponds, the Nipmucks beat their drums all night in mournful prayer. Even after the White Man came and settled the region alongside the Nipmucks, the lights continued to visit the area. The eerie chants and drums were unsettling to the colonists, who latched their doors, shuttered their windows and huddled close to each other until the morning sun brought peace, quiet and safety.

To this day, every seven years, the lights that are now called the Nipmuck Fishing Fires appear over the forests and swamps of the region. It is believed that the angry ghosts of the Narragansetts are still in search of their killers and the blue and yellow lights are their spirits wandering among the water and woods, forever searching for peace.

THE GHOST DOG

A rather unusual ghost haunts a certain section of Berkley, Massachusetts, once a part of the city of Taunton. The ghost is not a tribal warrior or a militiaman—in fact, it is not even human but rather the ghost of a dog.

The dog belonged to an Englishman called Edward Bobet (later spelled Bobbett, but state records spell it Bobet) who lived in that section of town. When war broke out in June 1675, Bobet feared his family might become casualties of the violent skirmish. Like many others, he decided to seek shelter, with his wife and nine children, in the fort at Taunton Green. On June 25, 1675, he and his family made haste to the shelter. Once they were safely secured, Bobet decided to return to the family home to retrieve some clothing and other provisions that would see them through a possible lengthy stay in the garrison.

Armed with his rifle and his trusty canine companion, forty-eight-year-old Bobet set out to gather the necessary belongings. On the journey to his homestead, he met with no confrontation, but the trek back proved not so fortunate. When he was within sight of the fort, a band of Indians spotted him and gave chase. Knowing his lone flintlock was no match for the throng that sought his head, he quickly eluded them and scurried up a tree in the hopes they would pass right by.

Once the enemy was within reach, Bobet's dog began barking at them and circling the tree. Unfortunately for Bobet, his dog had barked up the right tree, for the enemy took aim and shot into the tree multiple times, killing him. When he failed to return to the fort, a search party set out and found his mutilated body under the tree. Bobet became the first casualty from Taunton in the new war. He was buried near where he fell, with a crude headstone to mark the spot. The headstone was later uprooted and put into a stone wall. It was later moved to the Old Colony Historical Society Museum, where it is now on display.

Bobet's resting place, in a private yard near Berkley Bridge, is presently marked with a bronze memorial tablet put there in 1911 by his descendants. His dog was also a casualty of the war and perhaps never forgave himself for giving away his master's location that fateful day. To this day, people hear a frantic, unearthly barking near Berkley Bridge at the site where the horrific event took place centuries ago. No one is sure if the dog barks out of remorse or is eternally looking for his master. The echoes of the phantom bark permeate the area when there is no living canine around to produce the eerie sounds in the night.

Edward Bobbett's grave marker, on the front lawn of a private home in Berkley, Massachusetts. *Photo courtesy of Arlene Nicholson.*

Cross Berkley Bridge from Dighton and turn left onto Berkley Street. The stone is in the front yard of a private residence. Please respect the owner's right to privacy.

THE CRYING ROCKS

At the edge of Cedar Swamp in Charlestown, Rhode Island, just north of the old Narragansett Indian schoolhouse, sits an outcropping of rocks called the Crying Rocks. The rocks are also located near School House Pond, where a Narragansett boy named John Onion once challenged the devil.

According to Narragansett legend, the woods are so evil that, as Jeff Belanger and Ray Auger put it on their podcast *New England Legends*, "nature herself recoils in fear." The evil acts that once took place at the rocks reverberate to this day, and the flora below sometimes oozes with the crimson-red blood of those who met their fate at the base of the outcropping.

The rocks are about a quarter mile into the woods from the old Narragansett church. It is there that the sounds of babies crying echo through the trees.

A Narragansett man named John Paul once told Ezra Stiles of the terrible fate that befell many infants at the rocks. Children born out of wedlock and those born with an affliction or who became infirm were brought to the rocks and left there to perish or were simply thrown over the edge.

Times were different, and the constant movement of the tribe to summer camps and winter camps, along with hunting, wars and other vigorous living, created little room for any weakness. Those who were thought to be frail and useless through severe birth defects or illness were left on the rocks. It is said that at one time, a mass of tiny bones could be seen gleaming in the sun below the ledge. Although the bones are long gone, the spirits of the children still linger about the area.

People wandering by the rocks get an uneasy feeling or hear the sounds of babies crying. If one should dare venture out between the dark hours of two and three o'clock in the morning, they may hear the restless spirits at their most active moments.

BLOODY BROOK IN DEERFIELD

One of the most devastating massacres the English suffered took place in present-day South Deerfield, Massachusetts. At the time, Deerfield was on the very edge of the Massachusetts Bay Colony and was not very well fortified, even though the land was rich in soil and gave forth many abundant food sources for the settlers. The Indians knew both these things very well and chose to use them to their advantage. The area was originally known as Pocumtuck, and it had been occupied by English settlers for only two years when the massacre took place.

Deerfield was to be evacuated and its people sent to a blockhouse in nearby Hadley. On September 18, 1675,* Captain Thomas Lathrop took a team of eighteen teamsters (wagoneers) and sixty-seven militiamen to reap the harvests in the fields of Deerfield. The garrison, though fortified, had no provisions to sustain the people for the winter. The men filled the slow-moving oxcarts with provisions and proceeded to bring them to the safety of Hadley. Also at that time, Captain Samuel Moseley was sent to the area to scout and protect the people of Deerfield. His scouts

---

* Old Style date. The change between the Julian and Gregorian calendars was enacted in various European countries between 1582 and 1923. The New Style date puts the event on September 28, 1675.

were not as surreptitious as the warrior coalition that stayed completely out of sight of Moseley's scouts and Lathrop's men. Neither party was at all aware that five to seven hundred warriors had been skulking about, keeping under cover so as not to give away their numbers. They were able to stealthily follow the group of teamsters and militia without detection, waiting for the perfect moment to ambush them.

When Lathrop's party came to Muddy Brook, they decided to rest and refresh themselves while the oxcarts caught up. The stream flowed through a small clearing with a floodplain on one side and a thicket surrounding it. They had traveled five miles from their harvest point and felt safe enough to put their weapons in a cart while foraging for berries and wild grapes. This would prove to be a fatal act on their part. The warriors, led by Sachem Sangumachu, along with Sagamore Sam, Muttawmp, Matoonas, Monoco, Annawan, Penchason and Tatason, were all part of the Pocumtuck Confederacy, composed of several tribes. At the brook, they made their ambush on the party. Within minutes, most of the militia and all but one teamster were killed, including Captain Lathrop. Moseley heard the fighting while patrolling nearby and rushed his roughly seventy-man militia to the scene to find forty of Lathrop's soldiers dead, along with seventeen teamsters. The warriors allegedly drew him into the fight by taunting him, saying things like, "Come on Moseley, you want Indians. Here are enough Indians for you."

Moseley's men fought valiantly with little gain. As the day waned, eleven of Moseley's men were killed, and it appeared that the confederacy was slowly surrounding them until a stroke of good fortune fell upon them by way of Major Robert Treat's militia and Mohegan allies led by Attawamhood. The numerous reinforcements drove Muttawmp and his warriors back into the woods. In the end, Lathrop and forty-one of his men and seventeen teamsters lost their lives in the ambush, along with eleven of Captain Moseley's men. The number of losses on the other side was never recorded and most likely will never be known. The Indigenous losses were speculated to be numerous as a result of their military engagement with Moseley, Treat and Attawamhood, but Philip's forces never revealed any numbers in order to shield their casualties from the English.

The next morning, Lathrop returned to the battleground to bury the fallen. The dead had been stripped of their clothing and valuables, and some had been mutilated. The little brook that flowed through the field now ran red with blood and from then on would be known as Bloody Brook.

A crude monument was placed there, possibly in the late 1600s, to mark the burials. Somewhere along the way, the stone was broken into two pieces when moved to make room for a house. The two pieces of stone were placed in the front yard of a home, then on a sidewalk and in a nearby barn. They were eventually reset in their current location on the east side of Main Street. The mass grave was exhumed around 1835 to ensure that the spot was in fact where the men were buried. A twenty-five-foot obelisk was put in place over the grave site commemorating the massacre and those who perished. The original broken marker is presently located on the front lawn of a home Main Street in South Deerfield, with the tall monument nearby. Strangely enough, on the same day the mass grave was discovered, another was found with the remains of ninety-six Native Americans, about half a mile southwest of the English burial site.

Soon after the massacre, Deerfield was abandoned, and the area stood vacant for seven years. Philip and his warriors proceeded to burn the empty village just for the fun of it. Those who survived spoke of the massacre. Robert Dutch was gravely injured during the attack. When Moseley found him, he'd been stripped of his clothing, hacked up and left for dead. He survived his wounds and went forth to live on. John Stebbins of Deerfield was the only person from Lathrop's party who came out of the ordeal without a scratch. He would return to service and later retire. His home was burned in the 1704 Deerfield raid and his wife and children taken hostage, but only a few of his family were returned when ransom was paid for their release. Henry Bodwell, John Toppan and Thomas Very were the other survivors of the massacre.

The violent tragedy that day left permanent psychic scars on the land that people still witness in the form of what may be residual haunts. People hear disembodied screams coming out of nowhere, echoing through the air. Other witnesses claim to have seen men in early colonial dress appear out of nowhere and then vanish. Gunfire and cries are heard, as if the battle is replaying itself over again. The brook passes under Main Street in South Deerfield at what was determined to be the exact spot where Lathrop's party crossed and was ambushed. This is also the place where the two monuments can be found.

The bones of those killed that day may long since have turned to dust, but their tormented spirits still cry for help, perhaps eternally reliving that dreadful moment. Increase Mather described the mass grave as "one dreadful grave." Between the two burial sites and the later raid on Deerfield in 1704, the town has a lot of haunts roaming its streets and burial grounds.

INDIAN CORNER

In the town of West Greenwich, Rhode Island, there is a place called Indian Corner. After the war, English settlers leased the land from the Narragansetts. In 1709, the Rhode Island General Assembly accepted the lands of what is now East and West Greenwich as a gift from Ninigret, then sachem of the tribe, as payment for military protection and support against other hostile tribes. From that point on, settlers flocked to the newly acquired open land. It was soon discovered that a relic from King Philip's War haunted a certain portion of a road that ran from West Kingstown all the way into nearby Wickford, Rhode Island.

Indian Corner Road was a main trail during the war. It was marked with a large boulder that stood as a beacon for travelers who traversed the road in the winter when the snow tended to cover any vestige of the path. The familiar boulder assured the wayfarer that they were on the right track in their journey.

According to legend, rumors circulated for many years that the bodies of several Narragansett warriors who were killed in a skirmish near the rock were buried there and the stone had been rolled over the grave to mark their final resting place. The early settlers were aware of this, which may have contributed to the naming of the thoroughfare.

Over the next few centuries, strange and unsettling reports of a headless torso rising from beneath the rock became common. The form, surrounded by an eerie bluish glow, would slowly emerge from the earth. It would wander the area around the rock as if in search of something and suddenly, in a shot, take off into the night sky, leaving nothing but a trail of blue haze in its wake. Witnesses who knew that fallen warriors were buried there concluded that one of them was not at peace, most likely due to the manner of his demise— he perhaps having been decapitated. His body not being buried whole after death may have caused his spirit to become restless in the other realm. Such accounts are common in the annals of ghost stories throughout history, and this case was obviously no different. Those who were aware of the angry spirit avoided that particular area of the road after dark, for that is when the headless warrior would rise and commence his seemingly eternal, fruitless hunt for his lost head.

A tale is told about a man who was traveling the road late one night when he saw something gleaming in the moonlight near the rock. It was mostly buried in the ground, and on digging, he discovered it was a human skull. Having partaken in his fair share of libations, the man, not in a proper state

Indian Corner Road sign in Washington County, Rhode Island. *Photo courtesy of Kelly Pincins.*

of mind, decided to take his newfound prize home. He presented the skull to his wife, who demanded that he take it from her presence immediately. He walked out to the back of the yard and perched it on a fence post, pending a decision about what to do with his find.

Later that night, a terrible storm rose, permeating the sky with fierce thunder and lightning. The couple sat up and listened as the dreadful storm wailed on. But there was another noise that they heard, one not caused by the storm. The noise grew louder as the storm waned, and soon the couple had no choice but to check on the origin of the strange din. They peered out the window, and there in the backyard, just outside the window, was a skeleton. Its movement was so desperate that its bones rattled furiously as it shuffled around as if frantically searching for something. The couple, frightened out of their wits, quickly closed and sealed the shutters, then hid from sight until the storm, and the hideous rattling noise, passed.

In the morning, all was quiet. The sun shone bright, and the birds were chirping happily in the trees. The man gathered up his courage and ventured forth to check the backyard, where he found nothing out of place—except for one thing. The skull he had placed on the fence post the night before was now gone. The headless skeleton had come looking for his missing body part and, on finding it, gone back to his resting place under the rock. This, however, would not be the end of the haunting of Indian Corner. People still witness a skeleton sitting on the boulder along the side of the road as if

Section of Indian Corner Road where the headless skeleton is said to appear. *Photo courtesy of Kelly Pincins.*

he is now guarding the resting place of the warriors that lie in repose there. Venture down the road and enjoy a short sojourn at Indian Corner. Who knows what you may see?

WOLF ISLAND ROAD

A section along Wolf Island Road in Mattapoisett, Massachusetts, serves as a grim reminder of a band of Philip's scouts who were, unfortunately, discovered and dealt with by the English most harshly.

Several Wampanoag warrior scouts were sent forth to spy on the English and return with any intel on their next moves. The scouts were captured and hanged from the trees. Their lifeless bodies were left there as a warning for the enemy to stay away. Since then, that area of the road has been haunted by the ghosts of those Wampanoags.

Travelers along that section of the road have reported seeing the eyes of the dead warriors peering out from behind the trees. The glowing eyes follow them like sinister beacons, watching the passerby's every move. The glowing eyes may be enough to make one shudder, but there is another facet to the haunting that is even more terrifying to those who witness it.

People passing through the area are also taken aback by the sight of what appear to be silhouettes of human bodies hanging from the trees. The ghastly shapes appear and vanish at random. According to one account, a woman pulled her car to the side of the road where the spirits loom, most likely to use her phone. Suddenly, a pair of legs in old-time Native American dress swung down in front of the windshield. Within a few seconds, the legs were gone— and so was the witness of the apparition as she sped away, never looking back.

These hauntings occur mostly in midsummer, about the same time the incident took place. Wolf Island Road is considered by some to be the most haunted road in Massachusetts.

WAILING BROOK

Wailing Brook or Haunted Brook, off Route 44, is another site of a tragic event that took place during the war. When the leaves rustle and the wind comes quick, the cries of a woman are carried through the air, sending chills down the spines of the receivers of the ghostly howls.

The story of how the brook came to be haunted is a lost memory to many of the eldest in the town, but old tomes tell the tale and a very humorous anecdote. Elizabeth Perry's *A Brief History of the Town of Glocester, Rhode Island* tells the story as such:

> On the road that leads south, about a mile from the village of Chepachet, is a brook that after much rain used to sometimes run across the road. Here it was said an Indian drowned his wife, and all noises heard at this place were believed by many to come from this distressed Indian woman still haunting the brook. About 1825 an intelligent lady of this town, and her cousin, Mr. Rufus Steere, were riding to their home from the village over this road, and carrying a bottle of beer undergoing the vinous fermentation. As they were passing the haunted brook, all at once there was a fearful, loud report, like a pistol. The gentleman exclaimed, "I'm shot, and I feel the blood running down my back; I am faint." The horse was made to go with all speed. They reached their home and found the feared pistol shot was the explosion of the beer bottle.

The exact location of the brook is vague, but seeing as there are only a few in that area, just follow one and listen for the doleful cries of a woman.

HAND ROCK

For several days in June 1675, a small band of Wampanoag warriors was seen roaming the bank of the Nemasket River in Middleborough, Massachusetts, directly across from a colonial fortress. Each day, some of the warriors came forth, standing at the edge of the river and taunting the colonists inside the fort. It was an effort to provoke an attack, but none of the people in the fort felt an attack was necessary. After several days of taunting, the English decided enough was enough. They recruited Isaac Howland, an expert marksman, to shoot at the tormentors. Historians are divided about whether he intended to fire a warning shot close to them or to actually shoot one of the hecklers.

The gun chosen for the task was called a Thomson (also spelled Tomson and Thompson) long rifle. It was named after John Thomson, who, when each member of his militia was required bring their own gun, brought along his personal rifle, which weighed almost twenty-one pounds and stretched seven feet, four and a half inches in length.

Howland took aim with the Thomson musket and fired, mortally wounding one of the warriors. It was considered an amazing feat for the time, as the distance was over 150 rods, or 2,475 feet, basically about half a mile. This was way beyond the accuracy range of an ordinary firearm of the times. The Thomson long rifle used in the incident now sits on display at the Old Colony Historical Society in Taunton, Massachusetts.

As the warrior died, he laid his hand on a large rock. For some supernatural reason, his handprint was emblazoned on the boulder. He was carried about three miles away and buried alongside his fallen fellow men. A shaman later blessed the rock, making it a sacred Native place. Since then, the ghost of the fallen warrior has been witnessed at the rock.

A man walking with his grandson by the rock was surprised to see his grandson waving at someone. When the man inquired who he was waving to, the boy told him an Indian was standing at the rock, waving back at him. Sometime later, the incident repeated itself when the boy, once again, began waving at the invisible warrior.

In 1821, according to legend, Major Thomas Bennett was plowing his land and suddenly came upon a spot where he unearthed human bones, a knife, a jug and a smoking pipe. It was concluded that these were the remains of the Wampanoag who was felled by the Thomson gun at the Nemasket River.

To this day, he still haunts the rock, perhaps because his remains were disturbed, or it may be that he is angry about the fact that the shot that ended his mortal tenure was thought to be impossible. Either reason, or both, may have caused his spirit to return to the rock where it now resides as one of the many ghosts of King Philip's War.

Hand Rock is located at Barden Hill off Route 105.

ANGEL OF HADLEY

The town of Hadley, Massachusetts, was settled in 1659 when a group of religious dissenters from Weathersfield, Connecticut, decided to form their own congregation and community. This peaceful band of men, women and children lived harmoniously with the local tribes until the outbreak of King Philip's War. At that point, all bets were off about when they were to be attacked.

In August 1675, the colonial military made Hadley their base of operations along the Connecticut River. Troops and supplies were brought in, and a stockade was built along a bend in the river, which served as a perfect vantage point for defense in case of an attack. Portions of the palisade have been the subject of archaeological digs, as it was reported to be one of very few remnants of the seventeenth-century military defenses that were once erected all about New England.

On June 12, 1676, Hadley came under attack, but the marauders were quickly dissuaded by an unexpected three hundred English soldiers and two hundred converted Indians. The warriors came upon three soldiers who had left the safety of the settlement unarmed. Two soldiers were killed while running back to the fortification, and the third later succumbed to his wounds. Swarms of warriors came out of the woods to make an assault on the town but were successfully repelled, as the English proved greater in number than expected.

This event was well recorded, even though some of the facts vary from writer to writer. One other, less recorded event took place on September 1, 1675, when the town first came under attack. For some reason, this assault has been the subject of controversy about whether it ever really happened and, if so, what actually transpired. There would have been good reason to cover up the event at the time, for the protection and preservation of the town and its people. Here is the legend of the Angel of Hadley.

On September 1, 1675, Indians staged a surprise attack on the settlement. At the time, the townsfolk were gathered at the meetinghouse for Sabbath and were not well armed. Very few men had brought their rifles with them on the Sabbath, which was common during those times; they would prove too few to provide an adequate defense against what was about to take place.

The enemy came pouring into the settlement, taking everyone completely off guard, and the congregation broke into a panic, feeling for sure they were going to meet their maker at the hands of the attackers. Suddenly, a grave-looking man with long white hair and a white beard emerged from one of the houses brandishing a sword. This sudden stranger commanded the people while wielding his weapon like a master swordsman. In no time, the strange man had turned what was the inevitable annihilation of the town into a victory, saving all and repulsing the adversary. Then the figure, who had appeared out of nowhere, vanished as fast as he came, leaving the people in complete amazement.

It soon was surmised that this savior of the people was sent from heaven to rally and protect them in their time of most dire need. Although many that day had no idea who this man was, history plausibly identifies the hero, later dubbed the Angel of Hadley. The "angel," historians claim, was a man named William Goffe. Goffe was one of several Puritan judges who, in 1649, signed a death warrant authorizing the beheading of King Charles I after the overthrow of England by Oliver Cromwell and his army.

In 1658, Cromwell died, and the throne was restored to Charles's son, who had returned from exile to take his rightful place as King Charles II. He made it top priority to find and execute all those who had signed his father's death warrant. Goffe, now a regicide (one who kills a king), made his escape to the colonies along with fellow judge Edward Whalley. They hid among their Puritan kinsmen in New Haven until the English got word of their whereabouts. They quickly left town and hid in a cave overlooking New Haven but were forced to evacuate due to the large number of wild beasts in the area. The cave to this day is known as Judges Cave.

From there, Goffe and Whalley fled to Milford, then followed the Quinnipiac River into the Connecticut River Valley past Hartford and eventually settled in Hadley. Reverend John Russell took them into his home, where they hid in seclusion for more than a decade. The Massachusetts Bay Colony, although mostly Puritan at the time, was still under the authority of the reign of Charles II, so their presence was a clear and present danger to the town. Very few knew they were there, and those few took the secret to their graves.

Ezra Stiles, in his 1794 book *A History of Three of the Judges of King Charles I*, states,

It was usage in the frontier towns, and even at New-Haven, in those Indian wars, for a select number of congregation to go armed to public worship. It was so at Hadley at this time. The people immediately took to their arms, but were thrown into consternation and confusion. Had Hadley been taken, the discovery of the judges had been inevitable. Suddenly, and in the midst of the people there appeared a man of a very venerable aspect, and different from the inhabitants in his apparel, who took the command, arranged, and ordered them in the best military manner, and under his direction they repelled and routed the Indians and the town was saved. He immediately vanished, and the inhabitants could not account for the phenomenon, but considering that person as an Angel sent of God upon that special occasion for their deliverance; and for some time after said and believed that they had been delivered by an Angel,—Nor did they know or conceive otherwise till fifteen or twenty years after, when it at length became known at Hadley that the two judges had been secreted there.

Stiles gave Goffe the cognomen Angel of Hadley in his book. Goffe was about seventy years old at the time of the raid. He had been a proven military leader in the English Civil War under Oliver Cromwell, as became evident that day.

Edward Whalley died circa 1675 in Hadley and was buried secretly in an unmarked grave. William Goffe is estimated to have died sometime around April 1679, as that was about the last time his wife, Frances, received a letter from him. He is thought to be buried in an unmarked grave next to his father-in-law in Hadley.

There is a memorial stone at 102 Russell Street near Whalley Street, where Whalley and Goffe lived in secrecy for more than a decade. The stone reads,

REGICIDES LT. GEN. EDWARD WHALLEY, MAJ. GEN. WILLIAM GOFFE, HERE FOUND REFUGE IN THE CELLAR OF THE REV. JOHN RUSSELL 1664–1676.

MASSACRE POND

In Scarborough, Maine, there lies a pond formed by a saltwater tidal lagoon. Such ponds are quite common in New England, but the name, Massacre Pond, makes one think there is a formidable legend to it—and there is. The pond is located at Prout's Neck Wildlife Preserve just beyond Scarborough

Beach State Park. It was the site of not one but two attacks on the English settlers in 1677 and 1703.

The 1678 Treaty of Casco supposedly ended the wars between the English and the Indigenous people, but attacks and skirmishes continued, especially in the northern New England states, long after. Unfortunately, many of the English either disregarded the terms of peace or were not aware of them. This caused continued tension and deadly raids throughout the region.

The first attack at Massacre Pond occurred in 1677, when forty settlers were massacred by the Indians. In 1676, Wabenaki leader Mogg Heigon had managed to seize Scarborough, and the poorly armed Black Point garrison and town were peacefully abandoned, but not for long. Captain Henry Jocelyn owned the garrison. Although he was a successful and respected man, he was not much of a soldier. When Mogg and his warriors surrounded the garrison on October 12, 1676, Jocelyn accepted his offer to peacefully abandon it. The Natives stayed for a short time, and they, too, soon left the garrison house and village about a month later.

A short time later, some of the former inhabitants returned with a large military force and took shelter in the garrison. Mogg heard the news and on May 16, 1677, decided to retaliate and once again seize the garrison and village. The English inside the garrison were well armed, and after three days of fighting, Mogg was killed by a musket shot from Lieutenant Bartholemew Tippen.

According to William Hubbard in his book *The History of the Indian Wars in New England*,

May 16, another party of the enemy resolved to try their valor once again upon the garrison at Black Point, not doubting but to carry the place with bold onset, which they made with much resolution and courage, for they assaulted the garrison three days together, in which space of time they killed three of the English and took one prisoner, whom as it is said, they miserably tormented. The garrison on the other hand, as stoutly defended themselves, by the courage and valor of Lieutenant Tippin, that commanded them, and at last made a successful shot upon an Indian, that was observed to be very busy and bold in the assault, whom at the time they deemed to be Simon, the arch villain and incendiary of the Eastward Indians but proved to be one almost as good as himself, who was called Mogg, that had been the author of much mischief the year before.

With their leader fallen, the rest of the warriors lost their courage and fled the siege in canoes. Some went eastward, while five of them paddled toward York, Maine. This small skirmish set the scene for a larger and bloodier battle that would leave permanent psychic scars on the land at Black point.

Squando assumed leadership of the Wabanaki and vowed to avenge Mogg's death. Squando was already an ardent enemy of the English, for it was the English who had killed his son and wife, causing him to put a curse on the Saco River, the same waters they met their fate in. He and his warriors returned to Black Point garrison, where through keen and cunning planning, he managed to lure almost one hundred men out of the garrison, many of them to their deaths. On June 22, 1677, Captain Benjamin Swett and Lieutenant James Richardson arrived at Black Point with a very young and ill-trained force of forty English and two hundred friendly Indians.

Swett's men spied what appeared to be some of the enemy milling about as if wounded and began pursuit. This tactic of feigning injury had been used to draw Captain Pierce and his men into an ambush in Rehoboth a little over a year before—which fact should have been remembered and heeded. While chasing after the enemy, Swett's men came upon a steep hill with swampland on both sides and found themselves in an ambush. Most of the young fighters scattered in panic, but a few faced the enemy with courage and resolve until they were all killed.

Richardson was killed in the ambush, while Swett, who bore twenty wounds, fought his way back to the garrison, falling just short of its doors. Sixty men in all were slain: twenty friendly Indians and forty English. The town was decimated. A marker for the garrison sits one-tenth of a mile from the post office on the Route 207 Extension. The place is now named Garrison Cove. Massacre Pond is also named after Swett's defeat. A common grave is said to lie at the southwestern corner of the pond, which is now a residential area. People report seeing misty figures moving about in the area where the grave of the fallen soldiers is said to be. Ethereal screams and cries emanate from the area as if that infamous day is being played out once again. The ghosts of those who fell that day are not the only ones who still roam the area of Black Point and Massacre Pond: a raid years later claimed twenty more mortal souls.

A new garrison was established in 1681, three years after the Treaty of Casco was signed but not necessarily honored. The fighting continued, but soon another party would enter the fray: the French. On October 6, 1703, twenty men tending their livestock were ambushed by roughly two hundred Wabanaki warriors. The only man with a weapon at the time was a retired Indian fighter by the name of Richard Hunnewell who had lost his family in an Indian raid years before. He, along with the others, was killed and buried near what was once called Great Pond and later renamed Massacre Pond.

Occasionally, the ghosts of those so brutally murdered many years ago are seen at the pond, wandering along the shore. One is easy to recognize. The ghost of Richard "Crazy Eye" Hunnewell is quickly discerned by the wound he suffered in battle, which led to his nickname. Hunnewell's ghost looks as he did when he died. His body was horribly maimed and bloody, like the others. The raiding party recognized him by his crazy eye and remembered that he was an Indian fighter and their bitter enemy. They may have gone a bit further in making sure he would never fight again by brutally mutilating his body. They may not have taken into consideration that his horribly maimed ghost would actually rise, on occasion, with the others who lost their lives that fateful day, to roam the land they once called home.

DEER ISLAND

Deer Island in Massachusetts was a separate body of land in Boston Bay just off the shore of Winthrop until a hurricane in 1938 filled in what was once called Shirley Gut Channel. The sandbar made the island more of a peninsula, but the locals still consider it an island for the sake of the historical record and in keeping with its name. The island spans 185 acres with an intertidal zone of 80 acres. Two-thirds of the island is now home to a wastewater plant that serves forty-three towns and cities in the commonwealth, making it the second-largest of its kind in the United States. The remainder is parkland, offering activities such as hiking, sightseeing, fishing, picnicking and jogging. The island originally gained its name for the deer that would swim out to it to escape the clutches of wolves that roamed the woods.

On October 13, 1675, the Massachusetts Council, fearing a possible uprising by the Christian or Praying Indians, ordered them rounded up and brought to the island. Somewhere between five hundred and over one thousand (scholars debate the actual number) were confined to the island with little food and shelter. When winter came, many died from hunger and exposure. Although they spent only six months in captivity on the island, hundreds of men, women and children were said to have perished from the brutal conditions they were left to endure. Of those brought there, very few survived and went on to live out the rest of their lives.

The Reverend John Eliot, the man who converted many of the families, was completely appalled by the government's treatment of these people who had become Christians and assimilated into English society. It was Eliot who translated the Bible into their native languages for them to read and understand. He felt obligated by God to help them and attempted to bring them food and other provisions but was thwarted by the townspeople, who had been brainwashed by the authorities to believe that the prisoners, even though they were converts, were still dangerous savages and should be killed like the rest of their people. Several times, the townspeople attacked Eliot, trying to overturn his boat and forcing him to return to the mainland. A plan to actually go to the island and execute the exiles was made by the townspeople but was never carried out.

Daniel Gookin mentions the following in his manuscript *An Historical Account of the Doings and Sufferings of the Christian Indians in New England in the Years 1675–1677*, written in 1677 and published in 1836 in the *Transactions and Collections of the American Antiquarian Society Volume 2*,

> *Joseph Tuckapawillin, minister and pastor of the church at Hassanamesit… was sent to Deer Island…. "I am greatly distressed this day on every side; the English have taken away some of my estate, my corn, cattle, my plough, cart, chain, and other goods. The enemy Indians have also taken a part of what I had; and the wicked Indians mock and scoff at me, saying, 'Now what is become of your praying to God?' The English also censure me, and say I am a hypocrite. In this distress I have no where to look, but up to God in heaven to help me; now my dear wife and eldest son are run away, and I fear will perish in the woods for want of food."*

Needless to say, the English atrocities left an eternal mark on the landscape of the island. Strange cries and wails in various Native tongues are heard where there is no physical person to create them. The sound of phantom tribal drums and chanting is also heard. The converts who knelt along the shores praying for their new god to save them are still seen and heard about the parcel of land called Deer Island.

One more note: the island would later become a quarantine place for thousands of Irish immigrants who came over on the "coffin ships" with many sick and dead trying to escape the great famine of the 1880s. Due to the countless deaths and dark events that took place there, it became known as Devil's Island. The island later served as an almshouse and a prison until 1991. Now the great egg-shaped tanks of the waste management facility hold dominion over the landscape, but it is the many ghosts of the people who died there that hold dominion over the island as a whole.

ABRAM'S ROCK

At the outset of King Philip's War, several tribes chose to remain neutral for various reasons. Most of the converted or Praying Indians sided with the English. Members of the warring tribes often dissented and pledged their allegiance to the colonies, much like the Tories of the American Revolution pledged their allegiance to the throne instead of fighting for independence. This is the legend of one of those dissenters, called Abram by the English.

Abram was a renegade Christian Praying Indian who deserted the Wampanoags in favor of siding with the English. Abram became very close friends with the English, so much so that rumors circulated among the Wampanoag that he even had an English girlfriend. This made Philip very angry, as Abram knew much of Philip's plans and strategies regarding the proposed annihilation of the enemy. Philip sought to take Abram back and sent a search party out to find him.

In the meantime, Abram had found a towering rock he used as a hiding place and lookout. The west side of the large boulder had a natural room formed by other large rocks. This was where he lived in seclusion for several months until he was found and captured. Philip, being merciful at the time, gave him a chance to live. Abram was given the choice of leaping from the massive formation three times or instant death. Abram chose to take a chance and leap from the rock. Some historians argue that Abram voluntarily performed the act as a testament to his loyalty to Philip.

Tradition says Abram successfully completed the first and second leaps unscathed, but the third one became his demise. Legend has it that his ghost can be seen leaping from the rock, then appearing again at the top for another leap. The third time the ghost attempts to leap, he vanishes. Perhaps he is still trying to complete the task he failed.

Whether or not a hike out to the rock reveals a ghost should not deter one from soaking up the history and atmosphere of the place.

Above: The caves at Abram's Rock in Swansea, Massachusetts. *Photo courtesy of Arlene Nicholson.*

Left: The legendary Abram's Rock in Swansea, Massachusetts. *Photo courtesy of Arlene Nicholson.*

Abram's Rock is located in Village Park behind the Swansea Town Hall and Library complex at 81 Main Street. The trail leading to the rock is easy, and there are signs to follow. The natural room formation is still there and is called Abram's Bedroom, as that is where he allegedly lived during his months in concealment.

THE GREAT ELM

Boston Common is the oldest public park in the United States. From the time William Blackstone (Blaxton) grazed his livestock there to the present day, the land has seen many changes and faces. There have also been many dark times in history during which the common was used for executions. A historic cemetery, the Central Burying Ground, graces the common along with plaques, a pond called Frog Pond, ball fields, parade grounds, monuments, a bandstand and even a visitor center. What one no longer sees is the fixture that was once the most foreboding sight in the common: the Great Elm.

The tree was once dubbed the oldest inhabitant of Boston and, at its peak size, stood over seventy-two feet tall with a girth of seventeen feet and its lowest branch twenty-two and a half feet from the ground. When the first settlers arrived in numbers, William Blackstone sold them the common and relocated to present-day Cumberland, Rhode Island. The tree became a focal point for corporal punishment dating to before King Philip's War.

The Great Elm was the most notorious hanging tree in the colonies. Many scholars reflect on the fact that the Sons of Liberty assembled there and that the Reverend Jesse Lee, a Methodist pioneer, spoke under the tree in 1790, but those events are overshadowed by the ghosts of many whose lives were cut short on the branches of the former landmark.

The Boston Common is full of ghosts, from two ladies in Victorian dress who stroll the paths to those whose graves were desecrated by the construction of the subway system. There are those whose remains repose in the burying ground, but their spirits do not rest. Then there are the ghosts of the many who were hanged or shot by firing squad in the common, many of them prisoners from King Philip's War.

When the English sent the Praying Indians to Deer Island for containment, one well-known and respected Nipmuck leader and medicine man named Tantamous spoke up about his and his family's imprisonment in a rousing speech to everyone on the island. The English, not happy about his audacity, had him severely whipped. This did not stop Tantamous, for he found a way to escape the island and did so with haste.

When the authorities learned of his successful flight from exile, they reached out to his son for help in finding the escaped leader, promising that no harm would come to Tantamous when he was found. The son agreed, and Tantamous was captured, marched to the Great Elm and hanged. Not only did the English break their promise to the son, but he and the rest of Tantamous's family were also rounded up and sold into slavery.

At least forty-five other Native Americans were hanged from the Great Elm in 1676. When it was used for public hangings, the condemned were often left hanging from the tree for long periods as a message to others. Although there were many hangings, legend has it that the great and powerful Tantamous and his people put a curse on the tree and the land surrounding it. Visitors often report seeing hazy, humanlike forms dangling from other trees in the park. Some have heard what sounds like a rope creaking as if swinging back and forth with the weight of a person on it in the area where the elm once towered majestically over the common. Others sometimes hear desperate voices or moans in the same area.

The tree, which graced the southwestern corner of Frog Pond, fell in the gale of February 15, 1876. A memorial plaque marks the area where the Great Elm once stood imposingly on the common. The ghosts of those who swung from the tree may still assemble to retaliate for their fate, especially Tantamous and his people, who believed in the English and paid the ultimate price for it.

HOCKOMOCK SWAMP

The Hockomock Swamp is a vast parcel of wetland located in the northern part of southeastern Massachusetts. The 16,950-acre wetland extends into Taunton, Raynham, Bridgewater, East Bridgewater, Easton and Norton and is considered the largest in the state—and yes, it is haunted. Although part of the Bridgewater Triangle, Hockomock Swamp seems to have a whole life of its own, therefore having a whole section of its own. Hockomock, in Algonquin, means "place of spirits" or "place where spirits dwell," which readily suggests that that the Indigenous peoples of the area knew that there were magical forces at work there long before the Europeans arrived.

It is also believed that the name may be related to the number of Native burial grounds dotting the swamp. Thousands of Natives are thought to be buried within the swamp area. Either way, mysterious occurrences have taken place in the region around the wetlands that cannot be easily explained. UFOs are a more modern sight, but a Bigfoot, giant birds (perhaps the infamous Thunderbird of Indian lore), unusually large snakes, cats, dogs and other strange creatures have been reported roaming among the thicket that surrounds the Hockomock Swamp. Many who have visited the land have witnessed the large creatures that have somehow made the Hockomock their home, eluding, for the most part, the public eye. Where did these giant specimens come from? Are they products of the area, or did they migrate there due to the mystical forces that some claim permeate the swamp?

Among the more prominent sightings are the ghosts of Native American warriors who fell during the battles that took place in the area during 1675 and 1676. The swamp was used as a fortress and strategic base of operations for King Philip to launch raids and attacks on the nearby English settlements. The spirits of those who perished there seem to be attached to the land where they fell and were buried, their ghosts forever reliving the battles that took them to the other side. The area of the swamp harbors their mortal remains and their spirit energy in eternal unrest. Legend states that the warriors' souls are restless due to the fact that Philip's belt, the sacred belt of the sachem, was taken by Benjamin Church at Anawan Rock and vanished, never to be seen again. Paranormal activity is forever to take place in Hockomock Swamp until the belt is returned to its rightful people.

Ghost lights are also seen in the area. Witnesses have seen them floating about before vanishing into the water. Claims of poltergeists and shadow people darting about the perimeter of the hiking trails are often made. Hikers often get the feeling they are being watched while on the trails. They become very uncomfortable and overcome by feelings of negativity, as if the spirits in the swamp do not want them there.

There is plenty of information available in books and online regarding the strange happenings and how to get to the swamp, and there are hiking trails that can be easily traversed by those who wish to perhaps experience for themselves the ghosts and cryptids that lurk in the place where spirits dwell.

GREAT SWAMP

Great Swamp in South Kingstown, Rhode Island, was one of the most important battles of the war. It would also prove to be the most nefarious and the bloodiest. The Narragansetts had signed a neutrality treaty with the English stating they would not get involved in the war, but at the same time, they felt obligated to help women and children from tribes who had been displaced during the conflict. Governor Winslow took this as a sign of treachery on the Narragansetts' part and ordered an attack on their winter quarters. He believed the Narragansetts were harboring fugitives from justice, those who had slain his people. Failure to deliver these "criminals" would lead to the horrific end. The fugitives in question were the Wampanoags, who were considered Philip's people and therefore dangerous to the English effort.

The troops mustered at Smith's Blockhouse (see Smith's Castle section) where Richard Smith observed that they were poorly provisioned and ill-trained.

On December 19, 1675, 1,150 English and Mohegans, with the help of a captured Narragansett named Peter, easily marched up to Conanchet's

Illustration of the Great Swamp Fight, one of the worst massacres of the war. *Public domain, from authors' collection.*

95

five-acre fort in Great Swamp. At first, they found it difficult to penetrate the fortress, but a Connecticut regiment found an opening in the rear of the fort and rushed in. The Indians immediately killed several of the English, including Captains Joseph Gardiner, Isaac Johnson and Nathaniel Davenport. The inhabitants of the fort were severely overpowered. That day, 97 warriors fell, and 500 to 1,000 women, children and other noncombatants were mercilessly slain, shot, stabbed or burned to death. Many of the Narragansetts were killed, taken prisoner or ran into the woods, where they succumbed to hunger or the elements. The brutal battle almost annihilated the Narragansett tribe. The colonists, although victorious, suffered greatly as well: 70 men were killed and 150 wounded. Many English officers were killed during this fight as they led the charge toward the fortress.

In the 1930s, the Narragansetts became aware of a ritual that was being celebrated at the monument each year in which non-Indigenous Rhode Islanders held a tea party at the massacre site. This was immediately halted, and in its place, an annual commemoration of the battle began: a ceremony initiated by Narragansett-Wampanoag tribe that includes ritual wailing by tribal women.

There is a great burial ground where the casualties of war were interred, and at night, disembodied battle cries, gunshots and screaming echo through the hours of darkness as the spirits of those who perished in the struggle reportedly relive their last mortal moments.

Great Swamp Management Area is now used for hiking and scouting. In the fall and winter months, hunters grace the woodland looking for game. A long catwalk spans a section of the swamp where one can meander and imagine how difficult it must have been to navigate the terrain, especially in winter. Many artifacts within the confines of the old encampment have been unearthed over the centuries, such as arrowheads and musket balls. And other artifacts, those from the other side, also linger within the management area. Ghosts of those who suffered in the skirmish are seen wandering throughout the swamp. Warriors in full war paint and battle dress are heard screaming battle cries and are sometimes seen flitting through the trees and brush. English militiamen and women and children who met a tragic end are among the spirits that still roam the expanse, eternally reliving their day of infamy. Hunters, hikers and park service people all swear to the unearthly phenomena lurking within these cursed woods. An obelisk has been set up in the management area commemorating the pivotal struggle of the war. The management area is open Monday through Friday, 8:30 a.m. to 4:30 p.m. Entering the domain after dark is absolutely not recommended.

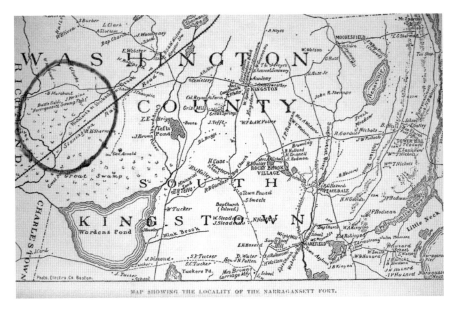

Map showing the location of the Great Swamp battle site. *Public domain, from authors' collection.*

Take Interstate Route 95 to Route 2 South and follow Route 138. Take Route 138 to Great Neck Road. Bear left onto Great Swamp Management Road. The road will end at a gate; from there, it is less than a mile to the monument.

SMITH'S CASTLE

One of the more prominent historic structures in Rhode Island was very well known during the war with Philip. It stands today as a monument to our history and haunts of the region. The history of Smith's Castle in North Kingstown, Rhode Island, goes as far back as 1637, when Roger Williams and Richard Smith established a trading post on the land for local tribes and colonists to barter goods. Williams, the founder of the Rhode Island Colony, thought it necessary to establish a trading post in the area in order to make friends with the Native tribes and exchange goods that would benefit both the English and the Natives.

Richard Smith Jr. migrated to present-day North Kingstown to build a home there. It was, at the time, called Smith's Blockhouse, located in what is still known as Cocumcussoc. Being on the water, it seemed perfect for trade until the outbreak of King Philip's War in 1675. There had already been Indian attacks on the land, and fearing for his family, Smith built tunnels that ran under the house and out to Rabbit Island very close by.

The trading post turned garrison became the base of operations for the United Colonies' Troops, including Massachusetts Bay, Plymouth and Connecticut, in planning and executing the attack on the Narragansetts at Great Swamp. The troops ate, drank, burned Smith's fence for heat and stole his articles and wares, all at the expense of Richard Smith, who petitioned the commissioners of the United Colonies for compensation. Lastly, Smith grieved how his home was burned to the ground by the Narragansetts in retaliation for the massacre at their swamp fort.

After the Great Swamp skirmish, the English militia hiked through the cold and snow to Smith's home, where many were nursed back to health but some, unfortunately, succumbed to their wounds and rigors of the brutal ordeal. Forty in all were buried in a single grave on the site. The area is well marked and easy to get to.

Another tragedy took place at the home after the fight. Joshua Tefft was tried and found guilty of treason for allegedly helping the Narragansetts during the confrontation. He was accused of warning the Narragansetts of the oncoming English, firing over the heads of the enemy as so not to hit any of them and helping them make their escape. Tefft reportedly wounded Captain Nathaniel Seely of Connecticut, who later died from his wounds. An Indian spy later told the English that Tefft did them a good service when he killed and wounded five or six Englishmen in the Great Swamp fight. Tefft was duly hanged, drawn and quartered.

Seventy men were ordered to remain behind, using the blockhouse as a temporary garrison. The day after they left, the Indians burned the house down in retaliation for the massacre at the swamp fort. The home was rebuilt in 1678 and has survived throughout the ages. In the eighteenth century, it became a thriving plantation and is now labeled the oldest in the nation. The property is also part of the Rhode Island Slave History Medallion program, which promotes public awareness of slavery in Rhode Island.

During the Revolutionary War, soldiers stayed in the secluded territory, and according to historians of the castle, a few skirmishes on the land resulted in the untimely demise of some soldiers during the war.

Combining the events of King Philip's War, the hanging of Joshua Tefft, casualties of the Revolutionary War and the residents on the property who died of more natural causes, it is inevitable that there would be a variety of ghosts lingering on the property. The ghosts of the property seem to be

Grave marker at Smith's Castle of the soldiers who perished in the battle at Great Swamp.
Photo courtesy of Arlene Nicholson.

trapped in an eternal struggle to right the negative energy that holds them to the homestead. Phantoms of people in colonial attire are occasionally seen wandering through various rooms. Some appear out of nowhere, then vanish as fast as they appeared. Various witnesses have seen a soldier in a Revolutionary uniform walking along the grounds near the water. Perhaps he met a sad fate at the house, or he is looking out to sea for something. His presence is semitransparent, and he seems to be unaware of any living beings who may be around him. Noises from inside the house give the curators and other guests a start as, many times, the noises emanate from the same room they happen to be occupying at the time. Voices and items falling are also heard by the docents, who wear period clothing most of the time to capture the mood and, perhaps, attract a few of the long-deceased tenants of the house. There are reports of phantom slaves who died while hiding in the escape tunnels below the house. The tunnels have long been closed due to their dangerously frail condition, yet the moans of the past and the apparitions of the slaves still permeate the walls and air of the ancient building.

There is one more account that is very arcane. This legend hails from the night after the Great Swamp Massacre. Some of the Massachusetts and Connecticut officers were having a drinking party in the dining room of the castle. Each one had a tribesman captured in the swamp fight standing behind him to be of any assistance while they drank their fill. Just as the clock struck midnight and after much drink, one of the officers, for reasons lost to antiquity, drew his sword and decapitated one of the enemy captives. The head rolled across the room, hitting the tall grandfather clock in the corner. The clock, on being struck, let out a loud ominous *bong* before ceasing to chime. From then on, the clock would strike only once on the hour, no matter what time it was. The clock was, at some point, repaired, but the unfortunate Native's spirit still lingers in the house. Sometimes the sound of something rolling across the floor can be heard in the dining room, as if someone is rolling a bowling ball toward the corner where the clock stood.

DEVIL'S ROCK

Natural landmarks are a commonplace sight in New England, from the ever-famous, now-defunct Old Man of the Mountain in New Hampshire to many lesser-known, even obscure sites. Some have a deep history, while others are steeped in legend. In many places, the devil left his mark as well. In Rhode Island, the village of Chepachet's name translates to "devil's bag." Legend says a Nipmuck was traveling the path Route 44 now traverses when he came across a bag of money. Knowing full well no one would actually lose such a large sum and not be aware of it, he surmised the devil had planted it there as a trap to lure in his next soul. The wise man dropped the bag and quickly vacated the spot, which would take on the moniker of Chepachet.

Devil's Foot Rock in North Kingston, Rhode Island, and Devil's Pulpit in Purgatory Chasm in Sutton, Massachusetts, are just a few places Satan has left his calling card. The list of places goes on and on; one could write a book in itself on such places that have been attributed to the Dark One. Devil's Rock in Portland/Old Saybrook, Connecticut, has an intriguing legend attached to it—for if one was to spy the indentation in the rock, they would have no doubt that the devil was once there.

In this particular place, the Natives held many a powwow while summoning the Great Spirit to make their crops fertile and their hunting successful in abundance. Then came the English encroaching on their hunting and planting grounds, making food sources scarce. The once peaceful powwows suddenly took on a more sinister tone, as they now included plans to decimate the evil intruders that sought to annihilate them from their native land.

When the tribes gathered at the meeting place on the Connecticut River for their next powwow, it was not for peace and good anymore but for the Evil Spirit to assist in completely destroying the enemy of their people. King Philip's War was in full force, and it was time to call on the Evil Spirit for help.

The powwow was held on the bank of the river near a great hole called the blow whence the Evil Spirit was said to rise. During the ceremony, water suddenly shot up from the hole like a geyser and began swirling. In the center of this watery whirlwind was the Evil Spirit, who had been summoned from his home below to be at their beck and call.

According to legend, one brave maverick did not believe in the existence of the Evil Spirit and that was the real reason the spirit came to the surface. The god was very angry about the brave's disbelief and, in an instant, grabbed the nonbeliever firmly and leapt onto a rock, leaving his fiery hoofprint emblazoned on its face, before jumping back into the hole with the young brave clutched in his arms.

Another account states that the Evil Spirit demanded a sacrifice for being summoned and chose the first person he saw. Either way, the young brave was never seen again, and the devil's footprint, resembling a cloven hoof burned into the rock, is visible to this day.

KING PHILIP'S DREAM

A well-recorded story, toward the end of the war, was told by Philip to his closest companions. He knew the end was near and that defeat was inevitable, but surrender was out of the question. The night before he perished at his home in Mount Hope, Rhode Island, he had a most disturbing dream. Philip was hiding out with some of his closest warriors in a cave in Norton, Massachusetts, when he had his vision of being slain by the enemy. The vision was so vivid that it became to him the ominous prediction of his fate.

Philip, a proud warrior and son of Massasoit, realized his fate was sealed and knew where it would play out. Because of this, he was compelled to return to his home, headquarters and throne to fight like a leader to the death. He was not to be taken alive, for he knew he would be put to death or sold into slavery, as his wife and son were when they were captured. Thus, he

The death of Philip. *Public domain, from authors' collection.*

had no more control over his destiny, which would be written about in books and articles for centuries thereafter. He knew he was to die like a king on his home soil. And so it was that Philip came out of hiding to fulfill the prophecy he had seen in that telltale dream.

He marched back to Mount Hope with dignity and pride. When approached, he fired his gun at the enemy, and when an Englishman attempted to shoot Philip, the gun failed to fire. It was one of his own, a Praying Indian by the name of John Alderman, who felled Philip with a single shot, just as he had seen in his dream. Philip met the fate he already knew awaited him from the dream he had the night before.

THE EDDY BROTHERS AND MASSASOIT'S GHOST

A very unlikely event pertaining to the ghosts of King Philip's War once occurred in Vermont. Seven miles north of Rutland, in a wooded valley shut in by the slopes of the beautiful Green Mountains, is the tiny hamlet of Chittenden. On a quiet back road, not far from this little community, sits a large, remodeled nineteenth-century farmhouse. The building, now in the possession of the High Life Ski Club, was once a center of communication with the spirit universe.

An attorney and former Civil War colonel, Henry Steel Olcott (August 2, 1832–February 17, 1907), while writing for the *New York Sun*, paid a ten-week visit to the Eddy family to find out once and for all if what he had heard was actually true: the Eddy family possessed an incredible supernatural ability to summon the dead. The spiritualism movement was at its height around 1874, and many claimed to have uncanny powers that defied logic and reason. Very few would leave a lasting impression in the annals of spiritualism with the otherworldly powers of mediumship the Eddy family proclaimed to possess. Although this narrative concerns two family members, William and Horatio, it is known that most of the eleven children had amazing powers inherited from their mother's ancestors. Olcott published his experiences with the Eddys in his book *People from the Other World* in 1875, giving readers the most complete perspective on what happened at the Eddy homestead before and during his tenure there. The book was a success, and people flocked to the little town of Chittenden to see for themselves the strange happenings that were transpiring in the old farmhouse.

Many others would witness the nightly exhibitions, and before long, the world knew of the Eddys. Their home became the spirit center of the universe and was often a subject of the *Banner of Light*, a weekly paper focused on spiritual happenings and philosophy in the nineteenth and early twentieth centuries. One interesting article regarding the Eddy manifestations came in two parts. A man named Henry LaCroix was among the guests at the Eddy home during a few sessions and chronicled his experiences. One of the more interesting portions of the narrative describes how several Indian spirits materialized, and one of them happened to be Massasoit. In part 2, LaCroix writes about the appearance of some of the spirits.

A goodly number of Indian spirits make their appearance here, but we heard none of them speak except one, who gibbered some of his idiom to a Mr. West. That class of control comes oftener, we are told, when the medium is unwell, or in bad condition, so as to give him strength. On Tuesday, August 3ᵈ, six of those Indian spirits appeared, attired in a gorgeous manner; some of their head-dresses were ornamented with beautiful flowing plumes, which they bent forward in the full light outside of the door of the cabinet. As one of them, called Massasoit, who came for a Mr. Tomson of Philadelphia, protruded his head outward, three beautiful pond lilies (of which none are to be found in this neighborhood) were seen among other ornaments on his head. Another, stranger still, who came to his medium, Mrs. A.W. Cutter, of Boston, had also a gorgeous costume and a Coiffure eclatante, (a brilliant head-dress), from which a seemingly living serpent, of the milk adder species, coiled around it, dangled his moving head over the brow of its charmer and possessor. Wickachee was the first to emerge from the cabinet on this occasion, and motioned Horatio to come on the platform. He was the only one who fairly and boldly walked out, and as he moved up and down on the platform, at first with his chosen companion and afterwards alone, we could but admire him and follow eagerly every one of his manly, bold and elegant motions. On leaving, he lifted his hand, a signal to have the full light for the exhibition of the others who were to follow him. Santum, on this and other occasions, filled the doorway with his great and imposing height. He was dressed from neck to foot in buckskin. Were we to interview the different spirits who came before our eyes, or even mention their names and those whom they came for, our article would surpass its bounded limits.

The Eddy family, mostly William, Horatio and Mary, were the center of attention for many years and still seem to be an enigma in the spiritual history of New England.

Zephaniah Eddy and his wife, Julia Ann MacCombs, had eleven known children: John Westley (born 1832); William H. (born 1832, died October 25, 1932); Francis Lightfoot (born 1834, died March 18, 1862); Maranda D. (born 1836, died March 29, 1871); Sophia Jane (February 2, 1840–July 18, 1913); Horatio G. (1842–September 8, 1922); Mary C. (April 1, 1844–December 31, 1910); James H. (1846–April 18, 1862); Delia M. (1849 [stone states 1853]–January 28, 1922); Daniel Webster (September 17, 1852–September 6, 1926); and Alice Julia (April 2, 1857–April 20, 1887).

All of them exhibited strange powers beyond rational explanation. Julia Eddy came from a long line of mediums and psychics. Her great-great-grandmother Mary Perkins Bradbury was tried, convicted and sentenced to hang on September 22, 1692, for witchcraft during the Salem witch hysteria. Somehow, perhaps by bribing the jailer or making a daring escape, she managed to gain freedom and flee to Amesbury. After the hysteria dwindled, she returned to Salisbury, where she died on December 20, 1700.

In their later years, at their home in Chittenden, William and Horatio began holding mediumship circles for spectators in a special room constructed specifically for that purpose. They opened their doors as the Green Tavern, taking in visitors to witness their shows. Six days a week, William would enter a small cabinet in the right corner of the circle room and fall into a deep trance. From there, various spirits would emerge from the box, singing, dancing and speaking to the crowd. Among them were William's mother, an Indian woman named Honto, several deceased neighbors and children and even deceased loved ones of the spectators who, in many cases, were unknown to the Eddy family.

Olcott arrived at the Eddy home on September 17, 1874, and attended a circle that very evening. The circles had become regular presentations at the home just one month before. Up to twenty-five people would be present on any given night. Among the spirits that appeared, Honto was the most frequent and entertaining. She was young with a dark complexion, standing about five feet, three inches. Someone suggested that a neighbor and spectator, a Mrs. Cleveland, check the beating of Honto's heart to prove she was real and not an image somehow illuminated through lights and mirrors. Mrs. Cleveland put her hand on Honto's chest. Her flesh was moist and cold and there was a faint but definite heartbeat. Her wrists also produced a pulse. Olcott, an avid investigator, noted very carefully all her traits and her physical demeanor during the ten weeks he witnessed the Eddy séances. Honto, along with most of the four hundred different spirits that emerged from the cabinet during his stay, bore no physical resemblance to William in any way.

Close examination of the cabinet and the room proved that no form of trickery was ever used. The cabinet was barely large enough to fit William, let alone a whole troupe of actors and the various garments they wore.

Two more Indian women of different appearance and dress emerged from the cabinet, one dancing and playing the violin. Olcott saw during his stay that William was neither musically inclined nor had any grace whatsoever when it came to dancing, as dances were occasionally held before the circles commenced. The Indian spirits were thought to be from the time of King Philip's War by their dress. Although they appeared quite frequently in the house, there was also a place out back in the woods called Honto's Cave where William and Horatio held a few séances.

At the cave, several Indian spirits appeared to astonished guests. Again, inspections and investigations into possible trickery were performed, with no conclusive evidence that the Eddy brothers were creating these spirits by some sort of illusion or using human actors.

Henry LaCroix arrived from Montreal, Canada, in July and was greeted by the Eddy brothers, who drove him and his traveling companions to their home seven miles distant. LaCroix would witness many other feats and acts of mediumship during his stay that left him awestruck. The fact that one of the spirits was labeled Massasoit is quite interesting. The article does not state how LaCroix came to know the spirit as Massasoit, as there was no known image of the great sachem to go by. This alone made his appearance monumental to the crowd. On finding out who they were witnessing, people now knew what he looked like. The ghost of Massasoit appearing in the Eddy home in Chittenden, Vermont, was a rather strange occurrence, as he lived his life and died near present-day Plymouth, Massachusetts. Yet that is who he claimed to be, and he carried on as such before vanishing like the other spirits that emerged out of nowhere in front of astounded guests.

Was it really Massasoit? This is a mystery in itself, which may never be solved. If it was, William Eddy was able to bring his ghost to life as he did with hundreds of other known and unknown people who resided on the other side of the veil.

CRYING BOG

The story behind the Crying Bog is illustrious and not without its share of variations. Regardless of the discrepancies in the story—based on who is narrating it, of course—the ghost of the Crying Bog has been seen since the days when people traversed the old paths either on foot or on horseback.

The ghost is that of a Narragansett Indian woman named Manouna who was exiled from her tribe after becoming pregnant out of wedlock. What made the situation even worse was the fact that she had fallen in love with a Frenchman and, much to her father's anger, courted him until they were to become parents. Unfortunately, when she felt the first pains of labor, she hid in a bog in what is now South Kingstown where she gave birth to two infant children. The bog was a forbidden place where no one dared venture because it was the hiding place of evil creatures that preyed on those who were foolish enough to venture into their depths. Unfortunately, Manouna had little choice.

As she stumbled through the fog and icy cold, the infants cried incessantly. Having just given birth, the young mother needed rest but knew she must carry on and bring her newborn children out of harm's way. As she pressed on, there came a voice that encompassed the bog around her, a voice that simply said one word: "Mine!"

Clutching her infants, Manouna ran until her legs could carry her no farther. She collapsed into a deep sleep. When she awoke, her babies were gone. She searched the bog until she finally succumbed to cold and weakness from her ordeal. Now, when the moon is full and the wind picks up, those passing by the bog can hear the cries of Manouna frantically searching for her two infants. One witness wrote many years ago of his ghostly experience while passing the bog during a full moon. As he and his horse traveled by, he suddenly encountered a woman sitting by the side of the marshy area, weeping. He stopped and asked if she was in need of assistance. The woman cried, "My children!" and vanished before his eyes.

Later, as the advent of the automobile brought motorists past the bog, witnesses described how they saw a woman in Native American garb sitting by the side of the road moaning, most likely for the loss of her children.

Another variation passed down tells of how Manouna strangled her two children. She may have killed them because she was banished from her village. She then buried them in the marsh to cover up her crime but soon became overwhelmed with guilt and took her own life. Her spirit now roams the marsh, mourning her misdeed. Either way, many witnesses still claim to hear her cries coming from the bog and report seeing her ghost near the side of the road moaning about the loss of her children.

Crying Bog is located at the corners of Route 1 and Route 108. Take Interstate Route 95 South to Route 102 South. Take Route 1 South into Wakefield.

THE MYSTERIOUS WALKER POND MASSACRE

History is full of missing facts and accounts that leave researchers scratching their heads about why there is no formal record. Sometimes it is because remote locations held no records of goings-on at certain points. Perhaps the event did not seem very important at the time but would prove to be noteworthy many years later. In some cases, the event may have been erased from history intentionally. In the case of the Walker Pond Massacre that took place in Brooksville, Maine, it would seem very hard to erase or forget to record an event that pretty much wiped out a whole Wabanaki village. Somehow, the incident became almost completely forgotten over time, and now, no one is absolutely sure when it actually took place.

Brooksville lies just south of Bucksport, near Deer Island. Walker Pond is a three-mile-wide body of water at the base of Caterpillar Hill. It is located near a place called Eggemoggin Reach, a watercourse that flows between Penobscot Bay and its scenic islands. Eggemoggin is named after a guide who was killed by the English after showing them where the Wabanaki were camped out.

There are several versions of what happened, each with a very different date: one says 1750s or 1770s, another 1704 and yet another 1660. A May 21, 1885 story in the *Republican Journal* out of Belfast, Maine, by Hosea Wardwell tells of what was known at the time as the massacre of Indians in Brooksville. If his story holds truth, the event likely took place either in 1660 or 1704. In his narrative, Wardwell states that the Puritans saw the Indians as a threat due to the fact they had embraced the Catholic religion as their faith. A certain Captain Cargill was sent to wipe out as many Indigenous people as he could. The article goes on to say,

> *Cargill surprised and captured a young Sanap belonging to the settlement of Winneway, and by the torture of fire prevailed on him to act as guide to the village of his people.*

After a long, tedious march, the English arrived at the village just as the day broke. Cargill's first order of business was to cut the throat of his guide, Eggemoggin, so he would not be able to scream out and alarm his people. The villagers had just risen and were preparing their breakfast, unaware of the peril that was about to befall them. Cargill's men surprised the villagers by firing on them with over two hundred muskets at once, killing almost all in the first volley. They then rushed in with knives and bayonets, finishing off those who had not already fallen.

Five hundred villagers were said to have perished, and not one Englishman suffered a wound. According to legend, only five escaped in a canoe to the east side of the pond: a French priest, an old woman and three papooses. According to the Natives, fifty escaped and joined their friends at Old Town. Wardwell states that a man from nearby Sedgewick had a great-grandfather who served under Cargill and put the event at around 1755. According to records, Cargill did destroy some northern Indians in 1755 and served two years in prison for indiscriminately killing friendly Indians as well. Records do not document the actual place. A man named Gray built a mill near the site in 1790 and employed a millwright from Massachusetts who recognized the place as one where he, as a private, took part in a massacre.

Another version of the story takes place in 1660, when famed Indian fighter Captain Benjamin Church led an expedition from Boston to Brookville in retaliation after a fishing vessel was taken and its men murdered. This same account is also told as the 1704 version of the massacre. The Indians had captured a fishing vessel in Eggemoggin Reach and burned it after killing all the fishermen aboard. News reached Boston of the incident, and Church gathered some men and headed north to Down East Maine.

Somewhere near South Brookville, Church captured an Indian scout and promised him his life if he would lead them to his village. The way was long and difficult, with Church's men traversing the wilds all night before reaching the village at daybreak. According to this account, the village was in slumber, unaware of the pending attack. All but one warrior is said to have perished in the slaughter.

The site of the village is still visible to those who explore the area toward the southern shore of the lake. Many artifacts have turned up, such as arrowheads, hatchets and human skeletons. An interesting side note concerns a widow, Grindal, who settled in the area around 1770 and planted a garden on the spot where the battle took place. She became accustomed to digging up the bones of the fallen villagers and piling them up until they reached the height of a large haystack.

Captain Benjamin Church. *Public domain, from authors' collection.*

All these dates and people seem to add more mystery to the matter of the exact moment the battle took place. According to researchers and historians, no records have been found that pin an exact date on the incident. The event took place, but when may always remain a mystery.

ANAWAN ROCK

King Philip's War, for the most part, came to an end at what is now known as Anawan Rock. Although the main fighting lasted for one year and two months, its toll was devastating on the colonists and, especially, the Indigenous peoples. The hostilities would continue for years after the surrender of Annawan, with the French siding with the Native tribes in another attempt to drive the English out of the region. Unlike in most wars, women and children were mercilessly executed on both sides when whole villages were raided. This was a war fought not for power so much as revenge and the obliteration of a culture.

King Philip, as the English called him, was eventually killed by one of his own, John Alderman, on August 12, 1676, effectively putting an end to the war. But two major players on the side of the Indians were still at large and wreaking havoc on the English: Chief Tisquapin and Philip's second-in-command, Annawan.

Captain Benjamin Church, an accomplished Indian fighter, was given orders to track down Annawan, who had safely fled the skirmish where Philip met his end. Annawan was an older man revered for his bravery and accomplishments in battle under Philip and his father, Chief Massasoit. It was known that Annawan had made it clear that he would not be taken alive by the English, and therefore, Church knew that he would have to create an effective strategy to beat the great warrior, who was now chief of the Wampanoags.

News traveled that Annawan was holed up somewhere in Rehoboth raiding neighboring farms for food. Rehoboth was established in 1643 as part of Plymouth Colony. Its boundaries were large and included present-day Rumford and Cumberland, Rhode Island. The English, while searching for Annawan, came upon some Indians skinning a horse. They captured them with no resistance thanks to the help of a scout who had come over to the English side. The ten men were brought to an old fort, where they were told that siding with Church would spare their lives. This, they decided, was a good idea, and they asked for their families to be gathered and brought to them. The ten had been part of Annawan's camp sent forth to gather provisions. They had been with Annawan the day before but knew not where he would have "kenneled" at present.

Based on the information gathered from his captives, Church set forth with a small band consisting of just six other men (one White and five Indian) to find the warrior chief. As they approached a swamp, they spied an old man with a rifle slung over his shoulder and a young woman. The old man was part of Annawan's council, and the young woman was his daughter. They had been sent to find the ten men who had gone for provisions. Church informed the man that they were safe in captivity and that his life would also be spared if the two cooperated in guiding them to where their chief was. The old man responded, "Since you have given us our lives, we are obliged to serve you" (according to Church's recollections in his memoir).

When questioned, both gave the same answer: Annawan and about fifty or sixty men were encamped in Squannakonk Swamp. When asked how many miles the swamp lay from their present position, the young woman answered that she did not know how to measure miles but that the swamp sat a good day's hike ahead. Church then inquired if they could make the swamp by nightfall, and the man answered that they could if they traveled steadfastly and stoutly. Church then decided that he would pay Annawan a visit despite his small band. The two captives had no choice but to agree to take the Englishman to the great chief.

On August 28, after miles of trudging through brush and mire, the group came upon the area where Annawan and his men bivouacked. Their camp was on the edge of a great rock, twenty-five feet tall and seventy-five feet wide. The old man cautioned them to wait until dark, as Annawan had sent his scouts out to ensure there were no enemies. When the last rays of daylight were well below the horizon and the scouts had returned to camp, Church's men carefully proceeded. Church asked the old man if he would fight on his side. The old man begged Church not to make him take up arms against his friend but then said, "I will go along with you, and be helpful to you, and shall lay hands upon any man that shall offer hurt to you."

Anawan Rock in Rehoboth, Massachusetts. *Photo courtesy of Arlene Nicholson.*

As they approached, they heard the pounding of a stone. It was an Indian woman pounding corn into meal. Church stealthily crept over the great rock with the old man and his daughter, and at one point, he could almost touch Annawan, who was resting with his son, both lying facing opposite directions. He noted that the men were broken into three companies and that they had used a felled tree lined with brush as cover. Their weapons, close to Annawan's feet, were leaning against a forked branch, with a mat placed over them to protect the flintlocks from dampness or dew. If wet or damp, the powder would not ignite, and the guns would not fire. Church realized that it would be almost impossible to mount an attack from his position. He asked the man if there was any other way in. The man told him that there was no other way in and requested that his warriors enter the camp by a small path leading to the rock, as anyone entering from any other direction would immediately be shot.

The men quietly retreated and came up with a new plan. The old man and his daughter set forth, with Church and his men crouching behind them. The party moved when the woman was pounding corn; when she stopped, they halted their advance. The trail into the camp ended by Annawan's side. The man and woman passed through uneventfully, and then Church leaped out from behind them, stepping over Annawan's son's head and taking up a position in front of the makeshift garrison of weapons. Annawan, both surprised and astonished, yelled in a deep, commanding voice, "Howoh!" Several contemporary texts state that the word means, "I am taken," but a translation by Roger Williams, who actually traded and conversed with the Indigenous peoples regularly, rendered it as, "Who is that?" This would make more sense, as Church initially startled him.

Church, taking their guns, demanded their surrender, promising them safe passage to Plymouth, where they would be spared. He instructed his scouts to go to the other two companies and tell them the same. The other companies also surrendered without a fight. Church kept up the ruse that a great army sat waiting in the swamp just outside the camp's firelight. Little did the Indians know that it was only seven men against the encampment of fifty or sixty Wampanoags.

The captain and his men had not slept in two days and had little to no provisions. Church said to Annawan, "I am come to sup with you." Then he asked what they had for supper. Annawan answered in a strong voice, "Taubut," meaning, according to Roger Williams, "It is satisfactory."

Annawan then asked if Church would prefer horse-beef or cow-beef. Church told him he preferred cow-beef. They supped together on beef

Above: The rear of Anawan Rock, where Chief Annawan and his men were camping out when captured. *Photo courtesy of Arlene Nicholson.*

Opposite: The capture of Annawan. *Public domain, from authors' collection.*

and mashed green corn lightly seasoned with salt, which the colonel had brought along with him as one of the very few provisions in his possession. When supper ended, Church asked his men if he might have the opportunity to nap for a few hours while they stood guard over the prisoners; then they would be able to sleep the rest of the night. Sleep did not come to the captain, as his eyes would not close. He sat up and noticed that Annawan was also awake. The two stared at each other for about an hour, not speaking, as Church did not know the Indian's language and feared that the chief knew none of his tongue.

At length, Annawan rose, threw off his blanket and proceeded into the woods. Church did not call out for fear of being thought of as apprehensive. He then thought that perhaps the warrior had a rifle hidden in the brush and began crouching close to Annawan's young son to shield himself from possible danger. According to *The History of King Philip's War* by Benjamin Church, Annawan returned with a bundle in his arms and, unwrapping it, said to Church in broken English, "Great captain, you have killed Philip and conquered his country, for I believe, that I and my company are the last that

114

war against the English, so I suppose the war is ended by your means; and therefore, these things belong unto you."

Contained within were the royal accouterments that Philip donned when sitting in state: the Wampanoag belt adorned with black-and-white beads fashioned into figures, flowers and wild beasts; another smaller belt with flags; and a small belt with a star. All three were edged with red hair from the heads of the Mohawks. There were also two fine horns of glazed powder and a red blanket. When placed over Church, the large belt stretched from his shoulder to his ankles front and back. These had been passed from Philip to Annawan, who would be the next chief. The two spent the rest of the night sharing stories of their victories and exploits as warriors.

In the morning, they proceeded to march to Plymouth. Church had promised Annawan's men that their lives would be spared but could not offer Annawan the same treatment, as he could not speak for his masters at Plymouth. He told Annawan that he would do everything in his power to beg his superiors to spare the warrior's life. While the rest of the prisoners were brought directly to Plymouth, Annawan and a few of his close scouts were taken to Rhode Island with Church to reside at his home for a few days before proceeding to Plymouth.

Anawan Rock sign. *Photo courtesy of Arlene Nicholson.*

Church was then ordered away to capture Chief Tisquapin and his small band, who raided farms and killed livestock and horses for food. After Tisquapin's capture, Church traveled to Boston. On returning to Plymouth, he became bitterly outraged at what he beheld. On the hill above the village were the heads of Tisquapin and Annawan, suspended from poles for all to see. It is said that Tisquapin claimed he was immortal and balls from a flintlock could not harm him, but when his assertion was tested, he fell dead from the first shot. Annawan was executed for brutality against the English, which he freely admitted. More than likely, the two were facing execution anyway for being ringleaders in the war.

The spirits of those who supposedly lost their lives during a battle that never took place (at what is called Anawan Rock) are reputed to haunt the encampment where Annawan and his men were captured. Visitors to the rock have heard the word *iootash* (Algonquin for "Stand and fight") reverberate through the sparse woods. Although there was no skirmish at Anawan Rock, some of the warriors may have yelled it in vain. In Church's memoir, he states that during the battle in the swamps near Mount Hope where Philip was slain, he heard a gruff voice shouting, "Iootash! Iootash!" several times—a verb in the second person meaning, "Fight."

Church did not know that it was Annawan who yelled the command at the swamps near Mount Hope. When he asked his Indian assistant, guide and interpreter, Peter, who the man was and what he was saying, Peter said he was Philip's great captain and that the word meant the men should stand to it and fight stoutly. Church, in his memoir, described Annawan as an "old surly fellow."

Regarding the other supernatural occurrences at the rock, some have even seen shadows flitting about the brush as if warriors from long ago were once again scouting the area for the enemy. Rehoboth residents sometimes see what looks like a campfire on the rock. When investigated, the ghostly fire vanishes. The smell of campfire smoke and the fire's glow are sometimes accompanied by the smell of cooked meat or, more grotesquely, rotting flesh. Others have experienced time slips and objects being moved. Strange chanting is heard reverberating through the woods around the rock. Numerous witnesses believe that the spirits of the Indians, perhaps even Annawan, have returned to reconsider their decision to surrender so easily and actually stand and fight.

RAYNHAM GHOST LIGHTS

The Wampanoags have their own version of spirits that loom over a certain area. The name given to them is Tei-Pai-Wankas. These are ghost lights in the form of orbs, spirits that remain as glowing orbs due to some sort of confrontation with a Pukwudgie (see section on Assonet Ledge and the Phantom Fires). People have experienced these strange lights in places where the mystical creature of Native lore has been spotted.

The Wampanoags have endured this small troll-like monster for eons, and it can be assured that a fair share of them met their fate at the hands of a Pukwudgie, thus accounting for the number of Tei-Pai-Wankas sighted around their old tribal grounds. One particular place where these lights are seen is behind the old Raynham Dog Track, now the Raynham Park Simulcast Center in Raynham, Massachusetts.

Every January, investigators and legend trippers flock to Raynham to see the glowing orbs that appear along the old railroad tracks behind the Raynham Park Simulcast Center. The dancing lights appear out of nowhere, then disappear again without a trace. The facility is located on Broadway in Raynham.

Elm Street in Bridgewater is also no stranger to these so-called ghost lights. The strange orbs are randomly seen along the street before mysteriously vanishing. Some have claimed they are nothing more than fireflies, but that is quite impossible, as that particular species of insect is not seen during the winter months.

The ghost lights are not the only paranormal entities at the simulcast center. It seems there may be a few Indigenous spirits lingering, perhaps eternally watching over their ancestors that float around the Hockomock Swamp near Raynham Park. Christopher Balzano, in his book *Ghosts of the Bridgewater Triangle*, mentions a gambler who spent much time, and more than likely much money, at the track. One evening, while leaving the building, he looked toward the swamp and saw what appeared to be an Indian, half naked, walking into the mire. It struck him as odd to see someone dressed so scantily for the time of year.

The gambler shouted out to the man that the swamp was haunted and that it might not be a good idea to venture into it. The Indian gave him a stern look, shook his fist at him and vanished into thin air.

LAKE NIPPENICKET

Another haunted place in Raynham sits on the Raynham-Bridgewater town line. Lake Nippenicket, locally known as the Nip, is very active with the spirits of the early inhabitants of the area. A large portion of the 354-acre lake rests in the Hockomock Swamp Wildlife Management Area.

Spectral fires and Native American ghosts are witnessed by those visiting the lake. Some believe that the lake may have been cursed long ago, causing an unusual number of drownings, boating accidents and people suddenly falling through the ice. What makes these tragedies so uncanny is that the lake is about three feet deep on average and, at its greatest depth, only six feet deep. The incidents have mounted enough over the years to force the town to forbid swimming in the lake. Fishing and boating are still allowed.

The lake is one of the most haunted spots in the famed Bridgewater Triangle. Everything from Bigfoot to giant birds and reptiles has been witnessed there. Legend trippers and cryptozoologists flock to the Nip in hopes of spying one of the many strange and elusive creatures that call the waters home.

The islands on the lake are said to be sacred places of the Nippenicket tribe, who once flourished there. There are alleged burial grounds of spiritual significance to the Nippenicket, and spirits of the Natives have been seen on the larger island along with phantom fires. When investigated, there were no people on the island and no signs of any fire that may have been burning. Phantom drumming is also heard on occasion.

The Nip is also said to be haunted by an elderly man who became one of the victims of the curse. He was out fishing in his boat, and when he did not return, it was discovered that he had drowned. His ghost is often seen by people visiting the lake at night. He silently paddles a small boat out toward the center of the lake before vanishing.

WADSWORTH CEMETERY

One of the more brutal battles of the war took place in Sudbury, Massachusetts, on April 21, 1676.

Historians believe the attack on Sudbury was more of a diversion to draw out the many militias that were stationed in the area at the time. It involved far more Indigenous warriors than would have been needed to take the town.

Captain Samuel Wadsworth and his men became unfortunate players in a battle that would forever be remembered. In George Bodge's book *Soldiers in King Philip's War*, he contributes a theory about why Wadsworth and his men may have suffered so many casualties that day.

> *Captain Wadsworth, with a company of some fifty or more men, marched out of Boston towards Marlborough that same day, expecting to make up the company to one hundred with the quotas of the Middlesex towns, but did not have over seventy upon his arrival…and these, many of them, mere boys.*

Marlborough had been attacked on March 16 and April 7, forcing most of the town to evacuate. The captain and his company passed through Sudbury on April 20, a settlement yet unscathed by the war. A large group of warriors gathered at the Nipmuck stronghold at Mount Wachusett and, after a conference atop Pompositticut Hill (now Summer Hill), decided to attack Sudbury instead of invading Concord, as was their original plan. The raid would be commanded by the Nipmuck sachem, Muttawmp, one of the fiercest leaders of the war.

Wadsworth and his men had left Sudbury to fortify Marlborough against further attack. In the meantime, a force of 1,000 to 1,500 warriors rained down on Sudbury on the morning of April 15, 1676. They burned houses and barns, killing several persons. Many of the residents fled their homes for the garrisons located nearby. Some were killed en route to the shelters. One house in particular, the Haynes garrison, held throughout the battle, despite attempts to burn it or infiltrate its walls. The foundation of this home can be found just outside the King Philip Woods Conservation Land.

An alarm was sounded, and on hearing it in the distance, a force of about a dozen Concord men rushed to the town's aid. Unaware of the magnitude of the enemy forces, they were ambushed within full view of the Haynes garrison; only one man escaped the massacre. The dead were buried in a mass grave just east of Old Town Bridge in Wayland.

Wadsworth's men also learned of the raid and marched toward Sudbury with Captain Samuel Brocklebank and his men. Wadsworth's men were tired, hungry and completely unaware of the enemy's position. About a mile from town, the militia spotted a number of warriors darting off into the woods. Thinking they had their adversaries, a chase began, but the men would soon learn it was a trap.

As the militia passed between Green and Goodman's Hills, out came the Indians in full force, surrounding the small, mostly untrained company.

Illustration of the Sudbury, Massachusetts attack. *Public domain, from authors' collection.*

Wadsworth fought his way up to the summit of Green Hill where his men formed a square, repulsing multiple Native charges. Any attempt at reinforcement by other English militia was ultimately repulsed by the massive number of warriors engaged in the battle.

The Natives set fire to the hill, causing Wadsworth and his men to choke on the heavy smoke and the militia to break ranks and run. Half of them were killed, including Wadsworth and Brocklebank. The rest managed to escape, except for, according to Increase Mather, five or six who were tortured and later dispatched. It became a commonly accepted conclusion that the men were captured, but Mary Rowlandson, a captive of the female sachem Weetamoo, was there at the camp and made no mention of any prisoners being taken. She did mention that the warriors, on their return, seemed more sullen than victorious. Rowlandson noted that it was perhaps due to the loss of some of their own. In her memoir, she states,

They came home without that rejoicing and triumphing over their victory which they were wont to show at other times; but rather like dogs (as they say) which have lost their ears. Yet I could not perceive that it was for their own loss of men. They said they had not lost above five or six; and I missed none, except in one wigwam. When they went, they acted as if the Devil had told them that they should gain the victory; and now they acted as if the Devil had told them they should have a fall. Whither it were so or no,

I cannot tell, but so it proved, for quickly they began to fall, and so held on that summer, till they came to utter ruin.

The soldiers who were slaughtered were buried at the foot of the hill. In time, a cemetery grew around the grave. The Wadsworth Cemetery on 74 Concord Road in Sudbury was named after Captain Samuel Wadsworth, leader of the twenty-eight colonial soldiers whom the enemy killed during the battle.

Three and a half acres contain an old section, a new section and areas for veteran burials. A monument marks the spot where Wadsworth and his men were buried. A slate tablet was originally put there in 1730 by Wadsworth's son. The obelisk was put there in 1852. The slate is still there as well.

The cemetery and monument are a favorite visiting place for empath Randall Parrish. Every time he visits the grave, he is overcome with a heavy feeling of sadness. He can feel the spirits of those who died in the battle centered on the granite memorial. Parrish describes the feeling as a "very old, foggy, overwhelming feeling that creates a loss of time in the modern world. It is a very somber feeling."

The cemetery is a stop for the Memorial Day parade where a ceremony is held to honor the Native Americans and the colonists buried there. The Sudbury Company of Militia and Minutes along with the United Native American Cultural Center come together and salute those who have passed. Drums are beaten, and a prayer bundle is placed at the monument by the cultural center. Then a final salute is fired by the Sudbury Militia.

SQUANDO'S CURSE

The Saco River originates from Saco Lake at Crawford Notch in the White Mountains, descending 1,500 feet as it flows through Harts Location, Bartlett and Conway before entering Maine. The river eventually flows into the Atlantic Ocean at Ferry Beach, where the twin cities of Saco and Biddeford are located. The river is host to one of the longest-lasting curses in New England—a curse that has lingered for more than three centuries.

The Sokoki tribe lived near the mouth of the Saco River. Their sagamore, Squando, was not only a young, strong, well-known and respected chief, but he was also a mighty shaman whose mysterious powers commanded great reverence from his followers. The Sokokis lived in harmony with the

White settlers in the area. In fact, it is said that Squando once rescued a young White girl from captivity and returned her to her family as a gesture of friendship and peace. According to the history of Saco and Biddeford, Maine, after a defeat during King Philip's War, Squando returned captives, including one woman named Elizabeth Wakely, taken at Casco, who was returned in June 1676 to Major Waldron as a gesture of peace.

Squando married Awagimiska and they had a son together named Mikoudou. When the war broke out, Squando and his people chose to stay neutral and at peace with their neighbors. One day, Squando's wife, pregnant with their second child, rowed out from Indian Island, now Factory Island, with Mikoudou wrapped in a blanket. Three English sailors had rowed upriver after mooring their ship at the mouth of the Saco. When they spied the woman and her baby, they sought to test the common report that Indian children could swim naturally from birth.

The three rowed their boat to Awagimiska's canoe and maliciously tipped it over, spilling Awagimiska and her child into the river. Another version says that one of the men wrenched the baby from the woman's arms and flung it into the rushing river. Awagimiska broke free from the men and dove to the bottom of the river to her drowning baby. Whether the men were surprised that the young Indian did not float is not recorded. The three men rowed off and soon forgot about the incident. Awagimiska saved her baby from drowning at that moment, but the child never recovered from the ordeal and died a few days later. Awagimiska became ill, and she, too, passed away along with her unborn child.

Squando became filled with a vengeful hatred toward the English. Wading into the quickening flow of the river, he held his arms toward the heavens and, summoning all his powers of magic, placed a curse on the White man that the river should forever claim three of his kind every year. He then used his powers of authority to rally his tribe to side with King Philip in the war against the colonies by uniting Androscoggin warriors in his cause. They raided colonial villages with vengeance and fire in their eyes, driving out as many settlers as they could. It was not only King Philip's war Squando now fought but also his own, in retribution for his family's death.

A treaty was signed in Cocheco on September 6 and in Boston on November 6, 1676. More terms were agreed on at Casco Bay in 1678 with Squando and other chiefs. One of the stipulations for peace was that the English inhabitants could return to their homes but had to forfeit one peck of corn from every household annually by way of acknowledgment to the Indians for possession of their land.

The treaty, although it reestablished some coexistence between the two cultures, did not lift the curse bestowed on the White men by Squando. Every year since that fateful day, the river claimed its bounty, sometimes even more than needed to satisfy Squando's wrathful spirit. People who lived near the river or knew of the curse stayed clear of the foreboding banks until the waterway had claimed its reward. In 1947, the front page of the *Maine Sunday Telegram* joyously proclaimed, "Saco River Outlives Curse of Indian Chief." It was the first recorded year that the mighty Saco had not claimed someone due to the curse, as there were no known fatalities from the river reported that year. This has not stopped Squando's curse from holding a fearful grip on those who dare defy the famous words of the angry chief.

Many who live in the region of the Saco River claim that the river and its curse still take its toll of at least one soul per year. To this day, Squando's spirit, still overlooking the Saco River, brings death to those who are not careful or respectful. Its prophetic past remains in the present and, perhaps, for eternity.

PARKER WOODLAND CAIRNS

The woods of the George B. Parker Woodland house a mystery that, to this day, no one has been able to solve. The land that the woodland sits on was originally purchased from the Narragansett Indians in 1642. The Waterman family became the second family to settle there in 1672. The land remained in the family for almost one hundred years before Caleb Vaughn became its owner in 1760. It eventually came into the possession of George Parker through a will. Parker later gave the land to the Audubon Society. After Parker's death in 1946, more property—including the Isaac Bowen house, from the early eighteenth century—was given to the society for public use.

The Isaac Bowen house is not the only house in the woodland. The remains of another farm sit off Biscuit Hill Road. The road got its name during the Revolutionary War when a wagon headed for General Rochambeau's camp overturned, spilling biscuits over the hillside.

The old home sites alone are worth the hike, but there is something even more interesting lacing the woods within the preserve. Mysterious cairns can be seen throughout the woodland trails. A cairn is a stone mound used by many cultures as a grave marker. Some scientists and archaeologists believe the many cairns found in New England go as far back as 800 BC, when the

Iberian-Celtic people and the Phoenicians were sailing to the present-day United States. Whoever built them stayed here for a while, because they are scattered throughout the region. Archaeologists can offer no definitive explanation for the origin of the many stone mounds. Some historians claim they may be ceremonial markers created by the Natives for rituals or rites.

Strange feelings and energy are reported to emit from the perimeters surrounding the cairns. People also get the feeling that they are being watched as they pass through the sparse woods where the many cairns lie. Those who claim to be empaths or sensitive suddenly feel a heaviness or even peacefulness in the air while standing near one of the ancient stone structures. A strange, faint whistling sound has been reported near several of the cairns. It resembles a barely perceptible howling wind.

The cairns in Parker Woodland are also thought to be possible Indian burial markers, which may explain the energy and feelings people get when near them. Others state that they are, perhaps, just rocks piled up by settlers clearing the land for possible future use. In many cases, farmers made what some call manure stones, or piles of stones placed in the fields for up to several years to help regenerate soil that has been depleted from overplanting. Sometimes these piles were never removed to become stone walls and were

One of the many mysterious cairns in Parker Woodland, Coventry, Rhode Island. *Photo courtesy of Arlene Nicholson.*

mistaken by subsequent landowners for Indian graves. Whatever the real purpose of the cairns may have been, they remain a mystery that is visible to the eye and, apparently, to the senses.

The preserve is located off Route 102 (Victory Highway) on the Coventry/ Foster line. Take Interstate Route 295 to Exit 6, Route 6 West. Follow Route 6 to the intersection of Route 102. Take Route 102 South. Bear onto Maple Valley Road, and Parker Woodland is well marked.

OLIVER HOUSE

Along the side of the Oliver House in Middleborough, Massachusetts, runs the Nemasket River. The river actually runs through the property, which is now a historic home and a very haunted one at that. The Peter Oliver House, located at the corner of Route 44 and 445 Plymouth Street, is one of the most haunted houses in the region. The home was built in 1769 by the Oliver family, who, being one of the wealthiest families in the colonies, hosted many dignitaries of the time in their beautiful home.

The Olivers were loyal to the king of England during the revolution. Because of this, they were forced to flee to Canada and, eventually, England. The home was confiscated and items sold to help pay for war expenses. It would eventually come back to the family in the 1940s. The home sits on fifty-four acres and is now a museum where tours are held and paranormal investigations are performed for a small fee.

The building is abundant with spirits from its past. Many people were born and died in the historic structure. Both residual and intelligent spirits are encountered by countless people. The ghosts of two women roam about the premises. One is thought to be that of Sally Hutchinson Oliver, the first occupant of the house. The ghost of a woman is seen at the top of the staircase leading to the second floor. This apparition has prompted several paranormal television shows to spend a night at the house in hopes of witnessing her on the stairs.

Disembodied screams, ghostly conversations and even voices interacting with the living are common at the Oliver House. One volunteer conducting a tour came face-to-face with a full-body apparition in one of the second-floor bedroom closets.

Ghosts of men and children are also seen wandering about the property. These are more modern spirits compared to the original settlers of the area.

Oliver House in Middleborough, Massachusetts. Up to 1,500 Indigenous people may be buried on the property. *Photo courtesy of Arlene Nicholson.*

Tree behind Oliver House where fairies are said to reside. *Photo courtesy of Arlene Nicholson.*

Before the Oliver family took possession of the property, it was home to the Wampanoags. The tribe hunted, fished and grew their crops on the land until it was taken from them by the English. Smallpox ravaged the tribe, and many died, almost completely wiping out the tribe. The land became a burial ground for the Wampanoags, and it is estimated that about 1,500 Natives were buried on or near the property. Some of the burial mounds can still be seen amid the thickets and brush that have reclaimed the land. The spirits of those tribal members are also thought to be among the ghosts that haunt the home. They may have held ceremonies on the property, conjuring up some otherworldly entities as well.

Reports of fairies or little gremlins reclining in a very old tree out back have also been documented. Some of the permanent residents of the place have been identified by portraits and photos, while others are still unidentified. Look up the Oliver House in Middleborough, Massachusetts, for more details and information.

KING PHILIP'S CAVE

One of the more talked-about locations within the Bridgewater Triangle is in Norton, Massachusetts, known as King Philip's Cave or Rock Cave (see section on Squaw Hollow and Rock Cave). This small, cave-like pile of rocks is where King Philip hid late in the war and where he allegedly spent his last night on earth before meeting his demise at Mount Hope. It was also where his prophetic dream led him to return to his home at Mount Hope to face the enemy on his own turf.

As the cave is a common stop for those adventuring within the triangle, many stories have circulated regarding strange and mysterious sightings. People have reported seeing odd balls of light floating about the area of the cave. These "spook lights" are known to appear and disappear at random. Campfires are also seen by those venturing toward the cave, only to vanish when approached. These are known as "phantom fires" and are seen in various places where Indigenous peoples' camps were prominent.

Others who have explored the area report the sound of phantom drumming, as if some sort of ethereal ceremony is taking place. The ghost of Philip is also said to roam the area he sought his last refuge in before meeting his fate at Mount Hope.

MOUNT HOPE, MIERY SWAMP AND KING PHILIP'S CHAIR

If there is but one single place King Philip would be destined to haunt for eternity, it would be where he sat at Mount Hope and the very nearby Miery Swamp where he met his end. The place where he sat and held council over his people is now called King Philip's Seat, King Philip's Chair or Seat of Metacom. The chair is a natural formation at the bottom of a large precipice at Mount Hope. It sits several feet high and dips inward on both sides, creating a natural seat. This was Metacom's throne, and when his final days came, he knew he had to return to where he was most respected and revered.

The day following his portentous dream, he returned to Mount Hope to face his final hurrah. Once there, he climbed to the top of the great outcropping that loomed high above his seat and looked out over the land he once ruled. A sadness like no other came over him. He then gathered his warriors and proceeded to Miery Swamp, about a third of a mile away. There, he began to plan any final assault or defense against the English. Unbeknownst to him and his men, the English were already hiding, lying in wait for a signal to fire on them.

King Philip's Chair at the base of a great rocky outcropping. *Photo courtesy of Arlene Nicholson.*

Sign leading to the Seat of Metacom, or King Philip's Chair. *Photo courtesy of Arlene Nicholson.*

When the melee started, Philip's warriors ran for the swamps, but Philip, knowing his end was near, ran toward the English and was felled almost instantly. On his death, the English beheaded him and chopped off his hands, giving the head and the scarred hand to John Alderman, the Praying Indian who shot him. Alderman sold the head back to the English, who later brought it back to Plymouth for public exhibition.

It was not enough, though. The English then had Philip drawn and quartered and, some accounts state, hung the parts in separate trees. Other accounts state they threw them in four different directions and left them without a proper burial, so Philip's soul would not be able to enter the land of the Great Spirit. Many Indigenous cultures believed that after death, the body, if not whole, could not enter the afterlife. Its spirit would spend eternity in search of its mortal parts in order to reunite them and move on.

There are many places where the ghost of King Philip is seen. Some claim he is looking for his head, which was sent many miles away from the rest of his mortal frame. If this is so, then his ghost may always return to the swamp to take refuge before embarking again on the search for his missing head and hands. A marker put in place in 1877 notes where in the swamp King Philip fell. The swamp is on private property deep in the woods where people rarely venture. It may be that his ghost roams freely there but unseen,

The killing of Philip by John Alderman. *Public domain, from authors' collection.*

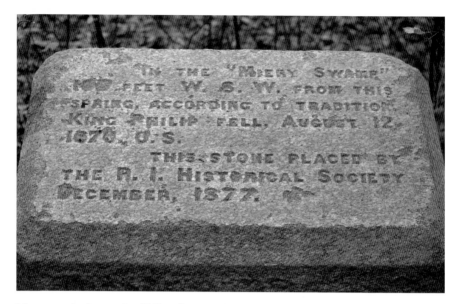

Monument in the woods of Miery Swamp where Philip was shot by one of his own. *Photo courtesy of Arlene Nicholson.*

because no one is there to lay eyes on it. Or perhaps the event is replayed as a residual haunting, much like at the battlefields of Gettysburg, Pennsylvania. Unlike Gettysburg, no one ventures forth to witness it.

There is a spring very close to where Philip fell that is said to be where he took his last drink of water, the last taste of earth's gifts before his eternal roaming. Maybe someone will be visiting the swamp and marker at the right time and behold the ghost of Philip either searching for something or reliving that fateful moment that changed the course of U.S. history.

The chair may be accessed by going to Mount Hope Farm on Metacom Avenue in Bristol, Rhode Island, and gaining permission through a parking pass. They will give you directions as well. The farm was actually part of the Mount Hope lands and site of an early Indigenous village where Philip lived.

PLYMOUTH TOWN SQUARE (KING PHILIP'S HEAD)

Plymouth, Massachusetts, is famous as the birthplace of the United States. Year after year, countless people visit the places and sites that mark the history of the town and the creation of a new nation: the *Mayflower II*, Pawtuxet/

Plymouth Village, historic homes, grave sites of the founding settlers, statues of both pilgrims and Indigenous peoples, Burial Hill and even Plymouth Rock, that perennial boulder (what is left of it) in the sand protected by a large granite canopy. There is one spot that is often sadly overlooked right within the town square. A small plaque commemorating an event Henry David Thoreau termed the "dark age of New England" sits on a small patch of grass near the John Carver Inn and Resort. It was there that historians say the head of King Philip was impaled on a pole and raised high in the square for all to see.

When Philip (Metacom) met his fate at his home in Mount Hope, the war was effectively over, at least for the English. Philip was beheaded and then quartered with a hatchet (see previous section) before having his head transported to Plymouth, where the magistrates could see for themselves that the great sachem had been killed. This was another brutal move by the English to avenge their people. John Alderman, the Praying Indian who shot Philip, was given the head and one of the hands with a scar on it, which he kept in a bucket and showed for a small fee. Increase Mather stated in his book *A Brief History of the War with the Indians in New-England*,

> He [was] *taken and destroyed, and there was he cut into quarters, and is now hanged up as a monument of revenging justice, his head being cut off and carried away to Plymouth.*

At the time of the militia's arrival in Plymouth on August 17, 1676, with their prize, the townsfolk were in prayer, giving thanks to their savior for delivering them from any more death and suffering. The head of Philip being raised high on a pole at the entrance of the village only gave the festivities more impetus. The head remained on the pike at what is now the intersection of Main Street and Town Square for roughly twenty-five years.

Several years later, Puritan minister Cotton Mather took it on himself to visit the site and remove the jawbone from the skull, stating this symbolically silenced the voice of the long-dead sachem. Some suggest his skull may have hung in the square for forty years or more, as the date it was finally taken down and where it may have ended up were not recorded. At one point, it was reported that wrens were said to have nested in the skull.

An interesting story is told in Edward Lodi's book *Ghosts from King Philip's War* about a family living in Raynham, Massachusetts, whose ancestors were friends with Philip. Supposedly, the family took possession of the head and hid it in their root cellar. During renovations of the courthouse

Plymouth Town Square where a plaque about Philip sits. *Photo courtesy of Arlene Nicholson.*

Close-up of the plaque in the Plymouth Town Square. *Photo courtesy of Arlene Nicholson.*

in Taunton, a pickled skull in a jar was discovered, sent to have its age and race analyzed and found to be that of a Native American. Whether or not it was the actual skull of Philip is a matter of conjecture, for this is also known to be a local legend.

What is not legend is the fact that Philip haunts the areas where he lived and his remains were left. The square is known to give off very unfriendly vibes at times, and people feel uneasy when there. The burial ground where reports say the head may have actually been hung is the site of the first Pilgrim fort. A tree there is believed to be inhabited by Native American spirits. This particular tree has roots that look like hands coming out of the ground and is thought to watch over visitors to the graveyard. If the spirits are not happy with a visitor, they will know by experiencing a terrifying feeling that suddenly washes over them. Reports of Pukwudgies (see the section on Assonet Ledge and the Phantom Fires) seen roaming the burial yard near the tree have also circulated.

The John Carver Inn near the town square is also rumored to be haunted by some very active spirits. Could one of them be Philip? No one is sure, but a short time after Philip's head was put in the town square, the heads of Annawan and Tispaquin were also displayed in the same manner. Tispaquin

Site of the first fort in Plymouth, Massachusetts, now Burial Hill. *Photo courtesy of Arlene Nicholson.*

was married to the daughter of Massasoit and, therefore, brother-in-law to Philip. He claimed he was a *powwau* (wizard) and that he was impervious to bullets. His men believed his assertion. Unfortunately, he was proven wrong when a single bullet felled him during his execution. If the ghosts of any of these three men were to haunt a certain area, the town square and its surrounds would be a major candidate. The area is also recognized for the brutality the English inflicted on these leaders. Perhaps that may bring some peace to the three who fought to save their land, only to suffer a horrible fate.

CHAPTER 2

THE GHOSTS OF
QUEEN ANNE'S WAR

As mentioned earlier, the Treaty of Casco did not end the war completely. Raiding parties continued to rain down on English settlements, except this time, the Indians had an ally in the French, who were also driven from their land by the English. For over twenty years after the treaty was signed, the English endured frightening and deadly raids by the enemies they thought they had driven out of the territory. As a result, some villages were completely destroyed and soon became a haven for the ghosts that still roam within their perimeters.

BETTY MOODY'S CAVE

Hostilities between settlers and Indigenous peoples were not confined to the mainland of New England. The many islands that were populated by the English also became targets of aggression by raiding parties. Among them were the Isles of Shoals, about six to ten miles off the coasts of New Hampshire and Maine. There are nine small islands in total, five of them belonging to Maine and four to New Hampshire. Before being discovered by John Smith in 1614, some of the islands were used as seasonal fishing camps by the Natives. By the 1620s, the larger islands were being sparsely settled by Europeans. Permanent settlements were in place by the time King Philip's War broke out but saw little to no threat—that is, until Queen Anne's War.

Sign for Fort Gilbert site in West Brookfield, Massachusetts. *Photo courtesy of Arlene Nicholson.*

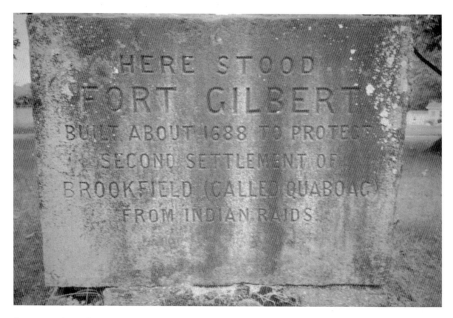

Stone marker where Fort Gilbert once stood in West Brookfield, Massachusetts. *Photo courtesy of Arlene Nicholson.*

In 1689, a band of Native warriors attacked Star Island, presumably in hopes of reclaiming their fishing camp. During the raid, a woman named Betty Moody escaped to a small cave with her two children. While holed up in the cavern, the children began to cry out of fear. Betty tried to cover their mouths so they would not be heard. Unfortunately, she covered their mouths so hard that she suffocated them. Some say she did it to spare her own life, while others believe she was so afraid herself that she was not aware of how tightly she was gripping their mouths until it was too late. Whatever version you deem valid does not take away from the fact that she appears to be eternally sorrowful for her deed, as screams and wails can be heard from the cave where she mourns her fateful act. The crying can be heard in the wind just before a terrible storm. Many say it is the ghosts of the children finally crying out. Either way, when the phantom wailing is heard and the winds pick up around the island, it is best to hunker down and listen for the echoes of the crying children or Betty to pass.

THE RAID OF YORK, MAINE

The year 1692 reigns in New England history as one of the most infamous. This was the year that the famous Salem witch trials took place, forever pushing any other event that transpired that year onto a back burner to be all but forgotten. Other events took place in 1692 that were extremely important to the region's history and, in some cases, horrendous enough to have those involved return occasionally to haunt the region where they met their fate. One such place is historic York, Maine.

On Candlemas Day 1691 or '92 (calendars varied), Abenaki Indians from Canada led by French officers raided York at dawn. Some three hundred colonists were killed or taken prisoner. The survivors were marched north into Canada while the village lay in burning ruins. Every building in the village was burned or destroyed except for three: the meetinghouse, the garrison house and the old gaol (jail) that was erected in 1656.

This event is overshadowed by the Salem witch trials later that year. History has a way of pushing aside some sagas to make room for others that coincide with the time frame they are latched onto. The spirits of the York raid, however, do not forget that fateful day. Moans can be heard at night from the graves and even cries of anguish. Strange misty figures have been seen near the common grave in both the pale of the moon and the light of

Left: York, Maine raid burial monument. *Photo courtesy of Arlene Nicholson.*

Below: Jeremiah Moulton's grave in York, Maine. He escaped captivity as a child and grew up to become a fierce Indian fighter. *Photo courtesy of Arlene Nicholson.*

day. They appear to be mourning the buried ones they lost so tragically. It seems that time is replaying those brutal moments that befell the village of York that horrific morning in 1692.

THE DEERFIELD RAID OF 1704

Deerfield was first settled in 1673 and became incorporated in 1677. It was then called Pocumtuck. This was a scant two years before King Philip's War and the first raids on the settlement. Englishman John Pynchon signed a treaty and deed to the land with some of the Indians, namely one called Chaulk, who had no authority to sign over any land and, more than likely, no idea that he was actually doing so. After settling the area, making it the westernmost outpost of the Massachusetts Bay Colony, the English proceeded to take more land. This eventually forced the Pocumtuck tribe to take refuge among the French. On September 18, 1675, a small band of Indians attacked and defeated a group of militias headed by Captain Thomas Lathrop. In retaliation, Captain William Turner and his men attacked a tribal camp at what is now called Turner's Falls on May 16, 1676, killing two hundred Indians, mostly women and children. The warriors returned to the camp to see the devastation and attacked Turner and his men as they retreated, causing more casualties for both sides. Turner was killed during the skirmish. This event took place during King Philip's War, but Deerfield, being an outpost colony, was prone to attacks even after the war with Philip ended. Queen Anne's War became a testament to that.

In the early hours of dawn on February 29, 1704, three hundred Abenaki and Kanyen'kehà:ka (Mohawk) warriors led by some fifty French military officers raided the little hamlet of Deerfield. The villagers were completely taken by surprise as, for some reason, the scouts and sentry had let down their guard. Buildings were burned, 48 villagers were brutally slaughtered and 111 survivors were forced to march in the snow three hundred miles north into Canada with mostly the clothes they had been wearing during the raid.

Reverend John Williams and his wife were fast asleep when the Indians rushed into their room. He grabbed a pistol and aimed it toward one of his attackers. The pistol misfired, which saved his life, for if it had gone off, the other Indians would surely have killed him. Two of Williams's children, six-year-old John Jr. and six-week-old Jerusha, were immediately killed in the

Grave of Samuel Allen, victim of one of the many Deerfield attacks; the inscription on the stone describes how he died. *Photo courtesy of Arlene Nicholson.*

raid along with one of their servants. Williams and his neighbors watched in fear and horror as the raiders killed many of the townspeople and set the buildings in the town ablaze. The villagers taken prisoner were forced to march for three weeks in deep snow and ice north into Canada. Because they were improperly dressed and had little to no provisions, many perished along the way. Those who survived were taunted for their religious beliefs while being shuttled from one settlement to another. It took a few years for Governor John Winthrop to gain the English captives their freedom. On November 21, 1706, fifty-seven captives, including two of Williams's children, arrived in Boston, redeemed. In his book *The Redeemed Captive Returning to Zion*, published in 1707, Williams depicts the horrors of those who were dispatched mercilessly for lagging behind or becoming a burden due to illness and hunger—one being his wife. John Williams later married his wife's cousin Abigail Allen and had five more children. He died on June 11, 1729, at the age of sixty-five.

John's wife, Eunice, having just given birth, was very weak when she was captured. Her strength soon failed her, and she fell a short time into the journey while crossing the Deerfield River. Her husband and children watched as an Indian dispatched her with a single blow of his tomahawk. Neighbors later found her and buried her in the Old Deerfield Burying Ground. A bridge now sits over the river in the spot where she died with a plaque that tells the story of the terrible ordeal.

When Governor Winthrop redeemed the captives, Williams's daughter Eunice, who was only seven years old when taken captive, remained with the

Grave site of the forty-eight victims of the Deerfield Massacre of 1704. While the massacre occurred after the signing of the peace treaty that officially ended the war, it was typical of the deadly skirmishes and raids that kept occurring for years afterward. *Photo courtesy of Arlene Nicholson.*

Indians. Within a year of her captivity, she had forgotten English. She later married a Mohawk named Aronson and changed her name to Kanenstehawi, completely rejecting the English ways of life. She died in 1786 at the age of ninety and was buried in Indian clothing. Some of her belongings are on exhibit in the Deerfield Museum. The book *The Unredeemed Captive*, written by John Demos and published by Alfred A. Knopf in 1994, tells the story of her life and the family's struggle to get her back.

John Stebbins, the only survivor to emerge unscathed in the Bloody Brook massacre during King Philip's War, was also taken prisoner along with his wife and six children. Although their home was burned, none of the family were killed in the raid or on the march north because John's daughter Abigail had married a Frenchman, Jacques de Noyon. John would later be one of the redeemed captives along with his wife and one son. The other five children chose to stay in Canada. He survived two enemy attacks while living in Deerfield.

This horrendous event left a paranormal scar on the village, especially the Old Deerfield Burying Ground. The female servant of the Williams family, Parthena, was pregnant at the time she was hacked to death with a

Marker for the home site of John Stebbins. He was only survivor of Bloody Brook to emerge unscathed and later survived the Deerfield Massacre. *Photo courtesy of Arlene Nicholson.*

Above: Grave of Pastor John Williams, the "Redeemed Captive" of the Deerfield raid in 1704. *Photo courtesy of Arlene Nicholson.*

Left: Grave of Eunice Williams, wife of John Williams. She was killed during the march to Canada after the Deerfield raid in 1704. *Photo courtesy of Arlene Nicholson.*

tomahawk and then scalped. Her ghost is seen and heard every leap year on February 29 near where she is buried. Unearthly screams emanate from the spot where her grave sits as if her spirit is reliving that dreadful day. The monument to the massacre sits in the far corner of the graveyard. Here, some still swear that the echoes of that fateful morning reverberate through the midnight air. The voices of those who were slaughtered eternally cry out in fright, perhaps looking for justice. One notable grave in the cemetery is that of a woman who died during childbirth. Sadly enough, the infant died as well. On the stone of Mary Harvey, there is a carving of her and the child in her arms lying in a half-opened coffin. The image is a bit macabre yet heartrending. The graves of John and Eunice are located under a tree near the center of the buying yard. Her stone reads, "She fell by the rage of ye barbarous enemy."

EUNICE WILLIAMS COVERED BRIDGE

Also known as the Green River Pumping Station Covered Bridge, the span sits near the site of Eunice Williams's demise during the 1704 Deerfield raid (see previous section). Eunice had recently given birth and was still recovering when the French and Indian raiding party attacked the village. Being weak and knowing her fate, she said goodbye to her husband and children, and while crossing the river, she lost her strength and was immediately hit on the head with a tomahawk.

When she was later found by the villagers, she was taken back to Deerfield for proper burial. Her remains are at rest next to those of her husband in the Old Burying Ground, but her soul or spirit seems to have remained where she met her fate on that terrible day. Her shade is frequently seen standing near the bank of the river looking out at the road. She is also witnessed standing on the covered span that crosses the banks of her demise. Passing motorists sometimes stop to help a woman in the river and get the scare of their lives when the figure vanishes in front of them. A man fishing once saw a woman standing near the opposite bank of the river. He walked past the side of the bridge to cast his line into the water. He then noticed she was not there but, in an instant, was standing right next to him. Startled by the split-second transportation of the woman across the river, he jumped backward. It was then he noticed something very wrong with her appearance. She was semitransparent, with a look of sadness on her face. Then, as quickly as she appeared, she vanished before his eyes.

The covered bridge mysteriously burned in 1969 and was rebuilt in 1972 into the ninety-five-foot-long, thirteen-and-a-half-foot-wide Howe truss overpass that extends over the site where Eunice William's spirit is to forever roam looking for redemption for her untimely death. On the bridge is a plaque recalling the raid that took place in 1704 and how Eunice Williams perished. The bridge is now closed for automobile traffic but can still be visited. Perhaps one may see the eternal resident that still lingers at the site.

THE SPECTER LEAGUERS

Everyone is aware of the Salem, Massachusetts witch trials that took place in 1692, but few have knowledge of an event that took place just north of the Witch City. This ghostly occurrence took place at the same time, and it was believed by many to be closely related. Author Samuel Adams Drake wrote of the physical phenomenon that plagued the town of Gloucester, located on Cape Ann, in *A Book of New England Legends and Folklore*.

> *It is gravely told in the "Magnalia Christi" of Cotton Mather, and on the authority of the Reverend John Emerson of Gloucester, how a number of rollicking apparitions dressed like gentlemen, in white waistcoats and breeches, kept Gloucester and the neighboring towns in a state of feverish excitement and alarm for a whole fortnight together.*
>
> *In the midsummer time, in the year 1692, Ebenezer Babson, a sturdy yeoman of Cape Ann, with the rest of his family, almost every night heard noises as if some persons were walking or running hither and thither about the house. He being out late one night, when returning home saw two men come out of his own door, and then at sight of him run swiftly from the end of the house into the adjoining cornfield. Going in, he immediately questioned his family concerning these strange visitors. They promptly replied that no one at all had been there during his absence.*

Babson and the rest of Cape Ann would be besieged for a fortnight by what they deduced were ghosts or specters, perhaps even demons in human form sent by the devil to torment them. Drake, along with Mather and others, also vouched for the authenticity of the event. Drake, in the aforementioned book, states,

> *But the fact that they were spirits, and no ordinary spirits at that, being so confidently vouched for, and by such high authority on such matters as Dr. Cotton Mather, would seem to dispose of all doubt upon the subject.*

Mather's account was written shortly after the event, using his own version in the telling, yet the conviction of his narrative has made the tale an integral part of New England folklore. He relied on the sworn testimonies of those who actually fought with the unknown assailants, who, in their conclusion, were not of this world. The men involved were of solid character and highly respected. For them to fabricate such a story would be detrimental to their caliber in society.

To continue the earlier narrative by Drake, Babson seized his gun and went in pursuit of the strangers. As he came upon a log, the two men jumped up and ran into the nearby swamp. As they ran, he heard one of them say, "The man of the house is now come, else we might have taken the house." In an instant, they were gone.

Stricken with fear of an attack by hostile enemies, Babson and his family took shelter in the nearest garrison. As they entered, the sound of heavy footfalls resembling an army marching around the house was heard. Babson and a few other brave souls armed themselves and sallied forth to confront the enemy. Instead, they saw the same two men fleeing the scene. It was then that they deduced they may have been French scouts and an attack was imminent.

The next night, Babson, being out of the garrison, saw two men whom he once again thought to be Frenchmen, as one of them had a bright gun, such as the ones used by the French Canadians, slung over his back. Both started toward him, but Babson was able to make haste to the garrison, where he got safely inside. Once again, the heavy footfalls commenced as if a league of men was circling the safe house. Babson and a man named John Brown spied three men outside and took a shot at them. To their surprise, the men dodged their bullets as if they were snowballs lobbed at them by a lame arm. For the next three nights, the three men, or what the townspeople now thought were demons or devils, continued to mystically appear here and there in attempts to lure the inhabitants from their safe haven in the garrison.

On July 14, the whole garrison spied half a dozen men who were now in gunshot range of them. Babson and his fellow townsmen set out in hot pursuit of the strangers. Babson saw two and took aim, pulling the trigger of his gun, yet it would not fire, thus allowing the two to get away. He then saw three more exiting the swamp, shouldered his rifle and fired at them. All three fell at once. Babson yelled to his companions that he had shot all three, but when he approached them, the three dead men rose and stole away into the night. One of them returned a volley that hissed by Babson's ear, implanting one bullet into a tree.

Babson and his comrades took cover and plotted another attack on where the specters were now concealed. Once again, the strange beings rose and retreated but not before one was felled by a shot from Babson's rifle. As they closed in on the casualty, they were seized by a sudden horror: the place where the enemy had fallen was void of a body. It was clear to the exhausted men that neither lead nor iron was useful against whatever monsters had come to torture them. No sooner had they reached the garrison than more were spotted roaming about the brush just out of gunshot reach.

The next day, Babson went out to the harbor to warn of the visitors and the danger that might follow. As Drake puts it,

> *While on his way thither he was waylaid and fired at by the "unaccountable troublers," who, strange to say, loaded their guns with real bullets, as poor Babson was near finding out to his cost. Having procured help, the neighborhood was scoured for traces of the attacking party, two of whom were seen, but not being of mortal flesh and blood, could not be harmed by lead or steel.*

For several days, scouts combed the vicinity of the garrison in search of the specters. One day, the scouting party spied eleven men departing an orchard where they had been performing strange incantations. Richard Dolliver fired into the assemblage, but as before, the bullets did nothing but make them scatter. It now became more evident than before, in Drake's words, that the "strange visitors bore a charmed life, and that the cape was in great peril from this diabolical invasion."

A regiment of sixty men from Ipswich was called in to assist in the fight against the unearthly visitors who, for a fortnight, had continually appeared in various places, harassing the people of Gloucester. Though they were repeatedly shot at, not one was killed or injured. The assailants beat on barns with clubs, threw stones, whooped and made various noises, resembling a poltergeist more than a foe wishing to annihilate an enemy. To make matters more supernatural, they left no footprints in the sands or swamps where they were seen and chased.

It was only a matter of time until the specters began confronting the soldiers of the garrison. Babson saw three of them one morning, walking toward him with no fear or apprehension. He quickly hid and waited until they were within stone's reach. He then shouldered his rifle and fired at them. The powder flashed in the pan, but no shot projected from the barrel. He tried repeatedly to shoot them with no success as the phantoms passed by without so much as flinching. He later was able to fire the gun several times in succession without fail. There was only one explanation Babson could come up with: the wraiths had charmed his rifle so it would not harm them.

In time, the visitors either grew weary of their diabolical pranks or perhaps had better things to do somewhere else. The odd happenings ceased as quickly as they had started. One account states that divine intervention played a role in their retreat.

It was decided that if mortal tools could not harm the specters, then the only answer was to pray to their savior for redemption from the evil. The people of the garrison converged and began praying for salvation. Their plan seemed to work, for not very long after, the specters were gone for good and the people of Cape Ann were relieved of the devil's minions that had, for some time, kept them in fear of being taken by the evils that sallied before them.

John Greenleaf Whittier wrote of the phenomenon that beleaguered the people of Gloucester in his poem "The Garrison of Cape Ann."

CHAPTER 3
INDIGENOUS LEGENDS

I n this chapter, some very interesting legends abound, compelling the reader to venture out and experience the places for themselves. Though not all of them are necessarily associated directly with King Philip's War, they are still an integral part of the perennial legend and folklore of our region. Each one seems to have some sort of moral that was well worth heeding for the characters involved and, perhaps, for those who became recipients of the orations.

JOHN ONION AND THE DEVIL

Just a short distance from the Crying Rocks in Charlestown, Rhode Island, is Schoolhouse Pond. The pond is frequented by locals who enjoy its beauty year-round. A story of the pond's darker side is told by locals and old-timers: the legend of a young Narragansett named John Onion.

John was a strong and brave Narragansett lad who was fond of visiting the pond, especially in winter when the frozen surface afforded him the pleasure of skating. John was fast on skates and always found the opportunity to challenge anyone who was there to a race. The result was always the same; John would outskate his opponent by a long shot. The other kids still often tried to race him but were no match for his strength and endurance on the ice. One evening, as the sun began to sink low in the winter sky, John, confident in his ability, yelled out to his friends, who had long since packed their skates and were leaving the shore for home, "I can never be beat on skates. In fact, I could outskate the devil!"

John continued his routine, and suddenly, from behind, he heard another set of skates. He turned around to see who was so close behind him but saw no one. John began skating faster and faster, but the sound of someone else on skates stayed right on his tail. Suddenly, he saw a dark figure closing in on him. No matter how fast he tried to skate, the figure kept gaining, skating faster and faster. John then remembered his words and, in fear, rushed as fast as he could toward the shore, where, in haste, he never removed his skates but instead ran all the way home with them still attached.

John never again dared to challenge anyone, especially the devil, to a skating match.

PURGATORY CHASM: MIDDLETOWN, RHODE ISLAND, AND SUTTON, MASSACHUSETTS

There are two known Purgatory Chasms, located in Rhode Island and Massachusetts, and several lovers' leaps strewn about New England that are associated with much the same legend. Some of these stories involve the devil, or Hobomock, as he is known by the Wampanoags, Narragansetts, Mohegans and Pequots, while others are purely born from forlorn or unrequited love.

The first site of legend is in Sutton, Massachusetts, called Purgatory Chasm State Reservation. The chasm is in a state park that includes hiking trails and offers picnic areas and a playground as well. This large chasm is a favorite hiking and climbing spot for many during the warmer months. With names like Devil's Coffin, Devil's Pulpit and Devil's Corn Crib, it can be assured there is a legend behind the land.

According to the legend, an Algonquin woman murdered a White colonial settler. The actual reason was lost to antiquity, but it is accepted that she robbed the poor fellow either before or after she did away with him. A short while after leaving the scene of the crime, she came across another settler, who asked if she could use company on her walk. The woman was very apprehensive because she had murdered one of his own. She began to run, but the man flew forward and grabbed her by the arm. The frightened woman began to call out to her Native American god,

Hobomock, for help but to no avail. The settler, with a sudden burst of fury, cried, "I am your god, Hobomock and I have come for you!"

He then threw his cloak away and revealed his devil-like guise. Grabbing his victim by the waist, he flew off into the air, landing on a rock formation, thus forming the chasm as he pounded the great formation with his cloven hooves, causing the rock to crumble underneath. He then threw the woman into the chasm and, with his tomahawk, cut large, deep gouges in the formation that visitors now attempt to squeeze through while hiking the chasm's trails. If you would like to see the work of Hobomock yourself, just take 198 Purgatory Road in Sutton, Massachusetts, and follow the trail into the great notch.

There is another Purgatory Chasm located in Middletown, Rhode Island, on the Newport border just off Tuckerman Road. This massive crevice is easy to get to and offers great views of some of the beaches in the area. There are several versions of a legend that surrounds this natural wonder. One of them concerns the headless ghost of an unfortunate Indian woman. According to legend, a local Indian woman killed a White man (sound familiar?), and Hobomock chopped off her head, then threw her off the 160-foot cliffs overlooking Second Beach. This was his reward to her for the terrible deed. He then sped away, burning his footprints into the top of the rocks. His footprints still appear in the rocks of the chasm.

Purgatory Chasm in Middletown, Rhode Island. *Photo courtesy of Arlene Nicholson.*

Another story tells of a White man and woman who were courting. The woman was a bit of a prude, and nothing seemed to satisfy her. Still, they were betrothed, and the man was bound by honor. One day, as they reached the chasm, she commented that if he was going to be good enough to marry her, he must first be able to leap across the opening of the chasm. Thus challenged, the man took his aim and leapt across the chasm, landing on the other side. Once he gained his footing, he tipped his hat, told her what he exactly thought of her and took off into the sunset. The woman never married, pining over the lost lover for the rest of her life.

The last legend is much like the previous one but concerns a young Native American woman and takes place before King Philip's War. This time, it is a young brave chasing the heart of the woman. He took her spurning him for only so long before he decided he was going to have her once and for all. One day, he saw her walking about and began to chase her. As they reached the chasm, the young woman made an all-out last-ditch attempt to leap the distance of the crevice. Fortunately for her, she reached the other side with no incident. Unfortunately, though, the brave did not and fell to his death. According to the legend, his ghost remains at the chasm, trapped for eternity chasing visitors who wander the wooded trails there.

Middletown is in the eastern tip of the state just north of Newport. Purgatory Chasm is located in the southern tip, called Easton Point, off Tuckerman Road near the corner of Paradise Avenue.

LILLINONAH'S LEAP

This next legend comes from the book *Ghosts of Litchfield County* and is called Lillinonah's Leap.

When the colonists were first settling the region, there lived a great sachem, Waramaug, chief of the Potatuck tribe. Waramaug possessed great skill, courage and wisdom far beyond his peers. The chief lived on a hilltop overlooking the Housatonic River near the present town of New Milford. His grand estate consisted of a great home twenty feet wide by one hundred feet long with many paintings on the walls drawn by artists from tribes near and far. It was known that this longhouse was the largest Indian dwelling in the region.

Waramaug had a beautiful daughter, Lillinonah, of whom he was most proud and loved dearly. Lillinonah was no less wise, courageous or skilled than her father. She was educated in the arts of social grace and diplomacy as well. When the young girl turned eighteen, word spread through the area, and young braves came from far and wide to win the hand of this Indian maiden. Alas, Lillinonah saw none of them as a fitting suitor; each in turn was sent away disappointed.

One cold winter day, Lillinonah was out strolling through the woods when she spied a handsome White man staggering aimlessly through the snow. She quickly realized he was disoriented with a fever and would surely perish if she did not act immediately. She helped the stranger back to her village, where she began to nurse him back to health. The long winter dragged on with Lillinonah constantly by her patient's side, keeping him warm and comfortable while he slowly regained his health.

Soon came the warmth of spring, and the Englishman was well on the road to recovery. The long winter had also brought a mutual affection between the two, and they soon fell in love. Waramaug, on hearing his daughter's wish to marry the Englishman, became angry and forbade their pending nuptials. If no brave was good enough for her, a lowly Englishman was most certainly out of the question.

Lillinonah rebelled against her father's decision in her own way by refusing to eat or drink. Her lovely features began to fade, along with her health. The chief, fearing she would not last much longer, thought it wiser to have a daughter married to a White man than no daughter at all. He finally consented, but before they could be married, the Englishman had to return to his own people to tidy up his affairs before settling down with his beloved to a new life among the Potatucks. He made plans to spend a final winter with his people and return in the spring to wed. Lillinonah waited anxiously for the arrival of spring and the return of her love, but when spring finally arrived, he did not return. Summer turned to autumn and autumn to winter, yet there was no sign or word of the Englishman's whereabouts.

Another year passed with still no word or news from her husband-to-be. Poor Lillinonah was heartbroken and began to show signs of failing health. Waramaug, in a last-ditch effort to find happiness for his daughter, arranged for a handsome young brave to be her husband. When Lillinonah heard of the secret arrangement, she became angry and quickly seized a canoe in an attempt to escape her prearranged fate. She furiously paddled down the Housatonic River toward the village of the Englishman.

The river was swollen, and the rapids required a death-defying feat to overcome, but Lillinonah, with the same obstinacy and courage as her father, feared not the imminent peril. The canoe rushed through the rapids toward the waterfall, with Lillinonah doing everything in her power to keep the boat under control. Just as she neared the falls, she spotted her love high on a ridge above. He had returned as promised and was on his way to her village when he saw the canoe barreling toward the falls.

The Englishman leaped from the overhang into the raging river below to save his love. Just as he hit the water, the canoe overturned, throwing Lillinonah into the rapids. He quickly swam to her and held her tightly in a loving embrace. Within seconds, the two were hurled over the falls, dropping to their deaths on the rocks below.

When the couple's bodies were found, they were still in an eternal embrace. Waramaug ordered them to be buried side by side on the top of the hill overlooking the Housatonic River in the area now known as Lover's Leap. When Waramaug passed away in 1735, he, too, was buried near his daughter and the man she loved.

Today, Lover's Leap State Park has easy access to the spot where people can stop and look on Lake Lillinonah, the site where the two lovers met their fate. There are the remains of a few buildings and an old factory. An old iron bridge leads the way to a few of the trails along the old Grove Street. The spirit of the two lovers and the chief are sometimes spotted on the ledge or in the woods nearby, wandering about the land they so loved in life.

NINEVAH FALLS

Killingworth, Connecticut, has an interesting historical account regarding another "lover's leap." The Hammonasset were a peaceful tribe that lived along the shores between the Agiciomock River and the Connecticut River. Their sachem was known as Sebaquanch, the "man that weeps." Uncas, the famous Mohegan sachem, wed his daughter and, by marriage, later inherited the Hammonasset land. He then sold a generous parcel of real estate to George Fenwick, Esq., of Saybrook. On November 26, 1669, Uncas sold the rest of the land to the residents of Killingworth. The remains of an Indian village are located about half a mile north of Route 80 near the junction of Roast Meat Hill Road and Wolf Meadow Road. The village consists of several rock shelters where Indian artifacts have been discovered. A place called Nineveh Falls sits not too far from the village within the Killingworth Land Conservation Trust near Lake Hammonasset. The area may have changed with the progress of time, but the tales of Indian spirits, witches and eternal love still reverberate through the history of the quaint town.

An Indian maiden became betrothed to a warrior who went to battle with a promise of marriage on his return. Sometime after his departure, news arrived of his death during combat. Heartbroken and distraught over the loss of her beloved, she walked to the falls and, in a state of depression and sorrow, threw herself into the rapids. The brave returned to find that his lover had received false news of his demise and, assuming the news to be true, leapt to her death. Knowing he could not go on without the love of his life, he decided to join her in eternity. He climbed the falls and jumped into the rapids in hopes of joining his bride-to-be.

To this day, when the full moon casts its soft glow of light on the land, witnesses sometimes see two ghostly figures walking along the edge of the falls, hand in hand in the eternal wedlock they were denied in life.

Nineveh Falls can be viewed from Route 80 in Killingworth for those who wish not to traverse the trails.

KENDUSKEAG STREAM TRAIL

Just about every state in New England has a lover's leap legend, most of them concerning a Native American and a European settler who fall in love but, somehow, things go awry. Maine has a very familiar lover's leap story associated with the Kenduskeag Stream Trail, which runs through the center of Bangor.

The story, like so many others, involves an Indian woman and an Englishman. According to the legend, the woman was named Tahalta, and the man went by the name of Shawano. Shawano was, by trade, a trapper who happened upon the young Tahalta one day. The two soon fell in love with each other, and after a short courtship, he asked for her hand in marriage. She was the happiest woman alive, dreaming of spending the rest of her days with the love of her life. She returned to her village with the news of her upcoming nuptials, but her father, the chieftain of the tribe, vehemently forbade her from marrying a White settler. He had already set plans in motion for her to marry a great warrior within their tribe called Kishwaukee. Tahalta would have none other than her Shawano, and so it was to be forever. Devastated by her father's decision, she returned to her fiancé and told him the news. Knowing they might never be together in life, they chose to create an eternal bond by leaping off the cliff hand in hand to their destiny.

BEAVER BROOK'S LOVER'S LEAP

The Beaver Brook in West Derry, New Hampshire, boasts a stone arch railroad bridge built in 1848. The area where the bridge sits has been known as Lover's Leap for generations. The legend associated with the area does not concern any lovers leaping to their deaths. Instead, this one has a happier ending.

In the story once reported by the *Derry News*, a Mohican Indian chief named Flying Cloud had a beautiful daughter whose name meant Bright Eyes. At the time, the area was known as Nutfield, and several tribes lived within the region. Bright Eyes fell in love with a warrior from another tribe called White Feather. Despite her father's attempts to find a suitor of his own for her, Bright Eyes had no interest in anyone else but White Feather.

This caused much distress within the family, as Flying Cloud despised her lover. One day he came upon them as they sat together on a hill overlooking the stream now called Beaver Brook. Flying Cloud, in a fit of rage, produced his tomahawk and began running toward White Feather with murder in his eyes. White Feather quickly scooped Bright Eyes up in his arms and leapt down the side of the hill to the brook where his canoe was hidden. They quickly made their escape to present-day Nashua, where his tribe was camped.

Flying Cloud soon realized that his daughter's happiness meant more than his desire for her to marry someone of his liking and sent a peace offering to the young couple, who lived happily ever after as husband and wife.

SHONKEEK AND MOONKEEK

This tale comes from Charles Skinner's book *Legends of Our Own Land*—the only tome in which it is known to appear. Its origins may be worth delving into for the detective of legends. The story involves two cousins, Shonkeek and Moonkeek, who grew up together playing in the woods, gathering nuts, flowers and berries. The two were inseparable, and soon, they realized they were in love with each other. The marriage of cousins was forbidden by Mohegan law, so when they reached an age where they could come and go as they pleased and began a courtship, they were quickly admonished and forbidden to be in each other's company. The two were not to be deterred. They met on an island in a body of water now called Pontoosuc Lake, located between the present city of Pittsfield and town of Lanesborough in western Massachusetts, where they were able to show their affection for each other without intervention, much to the ire and torment of one Nockawando. Nockawando, who wished to wed Moonkeek himself, tried everything to stop the couple's frequent rendezvous, including reporting her conduct to her parents. The couple agreed to elope to an eastern tribe, hoping to be adopted and live their lives free of harassment and shame. They made a pact to meet at the island, but if some sort of circumstance intervened with their plan, they would meet beneath the lake—or, in other words, drown themselves.

The next night, Shonkeek rowed out to the island where Moonkeek waited for his arrival. He did not notice Nockawando silently rowing in his wake. When Nockawando got close enough, he fired an arrow into the back of Shonkeek, who silently fell into the water. Nockawando swore he saw his foe fall out of the canoe, but suddenly, there he was sitting upright and rowing forward toward the island. Moonkeek saw the canoe of Shonkeek approaching rapidly, yet no oar broke the water to propel it. She leapt into her own canoe and pushed off from the shore. Moments later, Nockawando heard the death song emanate from the mouth of Moonkeek. He rowed forward to reach her but was suddenly grasped with a fit of palsy as his arms went limp.

As Skinner relates in his book,

> *The song ended and the night had become strangely, horribly still. Not a chirp of cricket, not a lap of wave, not a rustle of leaf. Motionless the girl awaited....It was no human creature that sat there. Then came the dead man's boat. The two shadows rowed noiselessly together, and as they disappeared into the mist that was now settling on the landscape, an unearthly laugh rang over the lake; then all was still.*

Naturally Nockawando was frightened out of his wits by this experience and ran back to the camp to tell his story. The tribe never found the two or any sign of their canoes. It came to pass that they believed the waters became a journey for the dead and so long as the lake contained its water, the lake will be a passage for those who pass into eternity.

WITCH ROCK

Witch Rock in Rochester, Massachusetts, has not only become a familiar landmark in the town, but it also boasts a very illustrious history. What one sees today is a more whimsical aspect that has been tended to for decades. The rock is adorned with the silhouette of a witch wearing a tall, wide-brimmed hat and flying on a broom. Under the figure are the words *Witch Rock* painted in bold, black letters. The rock is shaded by some trees, on the north side of New Bedford Road just as it intersects Vaughan Hill Road. It is located on private property but can be easily viewed from the street.

The legend of this rock hails to when Europeans first arrived in the New World. The Sippican Indians believed that evil spirits would rise up from the large split in the rock and wreak havoc on them; therefore, they avoided meeting or stopping at that spot. The colonists, fearful of witches and sorcery, believed that witches would rise from the rock on the full moon. During the war with King Philip, the rock became taboo and shunned by the English for fear the local Indigenous tribe had placed a curse on it, rendering a most horrible fate for any settler who dare pass within several feet of it.

There is another story of a woman being murdered at the rock. A woman accused of witchcraft fled Salem during the witch trials. By the time she got to the rock, her captors had overtaken her, and they killed her on the very spot where the rock sits.

The original idea to paint the witch on the face of the boulder came from Shirley Thompson in the 1950s. Thompson was a talented artist who had heard the many legends associated with the rock and decided to give it a proper moniker and logo. The home, known as the Thompson home to locals, was once called Witch Cottage. It has since become a landmark, serving as a guidepost for travelers along the New Bedford Road. There are more such landmarks in New England. Just because they appeared to be out of the ordinary or in a strange setting, they were believed to be evil omens. Such relics truly shed light on how the Native Americans and the early colonists feared the dark side.

ALEXANDER LAKE

The word *Nipmuck* (Nipmuc, Nipmuk) basically translates to "freshwater people." The tribe, being located near freshwater ponds and streams, gained a talent and, fortunately, the taste for acquiring and preparing freshwater fish. This fondness for fish outweighed their appetite for meat, and they found themselves trading corn and game with the Narragansetts for their versions of aquatic cuisine. The Narragansetts, aware of the Nipmucks' flair for shellfish and bluefish, sent forth an invitation for the two tribes to join in a feast. Both parties united in merriment, taking in food and fun, with fresh- and saltwater seafood abundantly overflowing from the tables.

Not long after the great feast, the Nipmucks returned the invitation to the Narragansetts, and another gathering was scheduled. The Nipmuck tribe prepared freshwater fish, corn, squash, beans and eels, while the guests brought their spread along with one of their own delectable creations: a special bread made from crushed corn and wild strawberries. The bread was presented as a gift, and the feast commenced.

During the feast, the Narragansett sachem noticed that the bread was never put on the table. Over time, he grew irate and felt insulted by the lack of interest in his tribe's gift. This led to harsh words, and within moments, a battle between the two tribes broke out. The Narragansetts were easily slaughtered as they had come in peace, without weapons. Some escaped to their village and declared revenge, but most died in the fight and were buried near the waters of the Nipmucks.

The Nipmucks decided to hold a powwow to celebrate their victory over the Narragansetts on the spot where Lake Alexander now sits in Danielson, Connecticut. There they set up camp and began a three-day-long gala where men, women and children played games, ate and drank without care or reservation. After a few days, the Great Spirit began to look unfavorably on the merrymakers, feeling the occasion had lingered on longer than it should have. The Great Spirit, already angered by the bloody squabble and treachery that had prevailed shortly before, decided to end their unruly merriment and mirth. While the revelers were deep in their celebrating, the earth beneath them began to give way, causing the deep underground streams and rivers to rise and flow until they flooded the whole area where the tribe had been whooping it up. Every man, woman and child was caught in the rushing waters and succumbed to the vengeful hand of the Great Spirit—all but one, that is. The very apex of the hill, where an innocent and devout old woman had been resting, was spared the wrath of their god. This island is now called Loon's Island and sits in the center of Lake Alexander. Whether or not the story is told exactly the same way is a matter of little consequence, for there exists below the surface of the lake evidence that lends credence to the legend. When the sun's rays beam onto the surface, illuminating below the ripples, there can be seen the remnants of the tall trees that once stood sovereign on the now-sunken hillsides.

WEETAMOO

The legends surrounding the death of Weetamoo have become more fashionable than the actual historical record. John Greenleaf Whittier wrote about her demise in his poem "The Bridal of Pennacook," placing her in the area of present-day Saugus, Lynn, Salem and Marblehead, Massachusetts. Charles Montgomery Skinner further perpetuated the legend in his book *Myths and Legends of Our Own Land*. Thomas Morton's *New English Canaan* contains a legend that may have sprouted the seeds that would be sown by later authors as the legend of Weetamoo. Weetamoo, according to recorded knowledge, never ventured that far north or at least never married and settled there.

Weetamoo (born in Tiverton, Rhode Island circa 1635–76) was also known as Wattimore, Weetthao, Namumpum and Tatapuanunum. She was a female chief of the Pocasset Wampanoag tribe and later became a war chief during King Philip's War. She was the daughter of the great chief Corbitant of the Pocassets. She married Wamsutta, brother of Philip, who had taken the English name of Alexander. She, along with Philip, became convinced that the English had poisoned Wamsutta after he visited the magistrates of the colony. They gave him refreshments for his journey home, and he died from a strange illness, much akin to poisoning.

Weetamoo would go on to marry five times. Her fifth husband was Quinnapin, the son of Niantic. Scholars believe this marriage was to drag the Narragansetts into the confederacy against the English.

Weetamoo would prove to be a great leader and warrior, leading some of the most devastating raids on the English settlements. Her most noted was the Lancaster raid of February 1676 during which Mary Rowlandson was taken captive. Rowlandson became Weetamoo's personal servant until she was redeemed later that year. Rowlandson described Weetamoo in the narrative she later wrote of her ordeal:

> *A severe and proud dame she was; bestowing every day in dressing herself near as much time as any of the gentry of the land; powdering her hair and painting her face, going with her necklaces, with jewels in her ears, and*

bracellets [sic] *upon her hands. When she had dressed herself, her work was to make girdles of wampum and beads.*

Shortly after Philip was assassinated in August 1676, Weetamoo drowned in the Taunton River while attempting to escape the English. One account states that she tried to cross on a fallen tree but fell into the thrashing current and so met her fate. She was feared as much as Philip during the conflict, and her death was considered a major victory for the colonists, who took her body and beheaded it, placing the head on a pole outside the fort in Taunton.

Her legend has survived centuries, with many places and sites named after her. Among the strangest are the places in the White Mountains that bear her name, like Weetamoo Falls, Weetamoo Trail, Mount Weetamoo and Weetamoo Rock. How did they come to be called so? The answer may lie in Whittier's poem, Skinner's retelling and Samuel Adams Drake's accounts dedicated to Weetamoo, even if they are not necessarily historically accurate. Here is the legend.

Winnepurkit, sagamore of the coastal settlements previously mentioned, married Weetamoo, daughter of Passaconaway, great chief of the Pennacooks. The couple honeymooned and returned to Winnepurkit's tribe to live out their happily married lives. After some time had time passed, Weetamoo wished to return to her people to visit and spend time with her loving father. Her husband not only granted her wish but also arranged an escort of his finest warriors to make sure she arrived safely. Once Weetamoo was safely home (near the site of present-day Concord, New Hampshire), the guards returned.

Time went by, and one day, Winnepurkit received news from Passaconaway through a messenger that Weetamoo wished to return, as she had finished her visit with her native tribe. The message went on to state that Winnepurkit was to send his guards to accompany her home. Winnepurkit felt his dignity as chief was slighted by this request. After all, he had been noble enough to send his men with her to Passaconaway; it would only be honorable for Passaconaway to reciprocate the deed. Winnepurkit sent a messenger back with the reply that included, "It stood not with Winnepurkit's reputation to make himself or his men so servile as to fetch her again" (according to Charles Skinner's *Myths and Legends of Our Own Land*).

Passaconaway, being a man of dignity and pride, was angered by this rebuttal. He sent a message saying that Weetamoo would stay where she was until Winnepurkit either sent some men for her or came himself to bring her back. As neither party would yield, poor Weetamoo remained with her father until enough was enough. The princess decided to take matters into her own hands and end the battle of pride and dignity being fought between the two men she loved most.

Legend states that, stealing away from her people, she launched her frail canoe into the Merrimack River, which at this time flowed with a wicked torrent. Unfortunately, she was instantly swept away by the rapids, never to be seen again. As Whittier describes it in his poem,

> *Down the vexed centre of that rushing tide,*
> *The thick huge ice-blocks threatening either side,*
> *The foam-white rocks of Amoskeag in view,*
> *With arrowy swiftness sped that light canoe....*
> *Down the white rapids like a sear leaf swirled,*
> *On the sharp rocks and piled up ices hurled,*
> *Empty and broken, circled the canoe*
> *In the vexed pool below—but where was Weetamoo.*

History can get convoluted over time. The Weetamoo of King Philip's War and the Weetamoo of the legend met their fate in the same way, but the latter has a more romantic story behind it. Perhaps there were two Weetamoos who, over time, became a legend of one. Whittier may have found more emotion in using the poetic license he was famous for. Either way, the legend of Weetamoo as told by Whittier makes for great reading.

THE LEGEND OF BALANCE ROCK

Balance Rock State Park is part of Pittsfield State Forest, located in Pittsfield and Lanesborough, Massachusetts. Within the confines of the forest is a natural oddity: a 165-ton boulder balanced on a bedrock slab. The stone is thirty feet long and fifteen feet wide and looks like it might topple over at any second, yet it has stood that way, precariously resting on its perch, since the last ice age. It has been a very popular attraction in the region for well over a century. Of course, there is a little-known Native legend about how it actually came to be.

It was at the site of the rock that one of the Atotarhos, kings of the six local Native nations, had his camp. He was a much-feared ruler who ate and drank from bowls made from the skulls of his enemies. He would cover himself from head to foot when visitors or messengers happened by. He was truly a ferocious warlord who let no one stand in his way. His son, on the other hand, was born with gentler tendencies and was almost feminine in his appearance and manner. On his succession to the throne, he eschewed war and violence and instead practiced peace and harmony.

The young Atotarho stood one day at Balance Rock watching some of the young warriors play a game called duff, in which one stone is placed atop another and the players, standing as far away as they can, attempt to knock the stones out of place with their own stone. As the girlish-looking Atotarho looked on, a few of the players made mockery of his demeanor and looks, challenging him to test his skill against theirs. The young chief took on the challenge, and the laughter and mockery turned to astonishment and fear, for each step he took, he grew in size until he towered well above their now-puny frames. They then realized who he was and fell to their knees in dread. Atotarho calmly lifted great boulders and tossed them around as if they were mere beechnuts. His last show of power was to lift a giant rock and place it gently on another, leaving it to balance precariously but solidly in its place, then cautioned them about ill manners and quick judgement. He then returned to his slender form, leaving the shaken players to resume their game.

For many years after, old tribal members related the story and its lesson about manners and wisdom from atop Atotarho's duff, now called Balance Rock.

To get to the rock, take Route 7 in Lanesborough to Bull Hill Road. Take a left onto Bull Hill Road then a right onto Balance Rock Road. The gate will be on your right. The rock is about a mile's walk in on a well-marked trail to the northeast corner of the park.

DEVIL'S FOOT ROCK

While one is driving on Post Road in North Kingstown, Rhode Island, a street sign may prompt a second look. It has the strange name Devil's Foot Road. The road was named after a granite ledge just past a dirt parking area. The legend dates to colonial times, but the actual rock was hidden in the wild until the building of a railway system nearby uncovered its whereabouts. The legend has a few different versions, as many of antiquity do, but the end result is the same.

Devil's Foot Rock in North Kingstown, Rhode Island. *Photo courtesy of Arlene Nicholson.*

One version is about an Indian woman who was chased by the devil after leaving Boston. During the early days of New England, many people left the Massachusetts Bay Colony to escape the religious persecution of the Puritans, hence Roger Williams and his band coming to the Ocean State to practice their own brand of religion. The woman, who spurned Christianity, was finally caught at the rock and scooped up by the devil, who, making a bounding leap, burned holes into the rock with his fiery hooves. This version may have circulated as a way of scaring the Puritan folk into submission.

Another version states that the woman killed a man in Wickford, Rhode Island, and while escaping, came upon a well-dressed gentleman walking in the same direction. When asked if she would prefer company, she told him no and tried to run, but the devil grabbed her and revealed his true identity before stomping on the ground, leaving his footprints in the rock. He then catapulted into the air with his prey, flew her to Purgatory Chasm and dropped her into the water (see section on Purgatory Chasm: Middletown, Rhode Island, and Sutton, Massachusetts).

One more legend is about the devil and his dogs roaming Rhode Island, looking for a bride. He spied a woman walking along the old road that is now part of the rock. Despite his best advances, she rejected him until he decided enough was enough. He grabbed her hand and began running up the rock, leaping into the air before changing into a serpent and landing at Narragansett Bay. While making his exit off the rock, he and his dogs burned their prints into the granite ledge. The rock still sits off Route 1 in North Kingstown. The hoofprints are as fresh as the day they were burned into the stone by the unholy creature.

Take Interstate Route 95 to Route 1 North. Just after you pass over the bridge of Route 403, there is a sandlot. Pull into the lot, and there is a path off to the right. The rock is a few yards into the woods on the path to the left.

BIBLIOGRAPHY

Balzano, Christopher. *Dark Woods: Cults, Crime and Paranormal in the Freetown State Forest.* Atglen, PA: Schiffer, 2008.
———. *Ghosts of the Bridgewater Triangle.* Atglen, PA: Schiffer, 2008.
Beers, J.H. *Biographical Record of Middlesex County Connecticut.* Chicago: J.H. Beers, 1903.
Belknap, Jeremy. *The History of New Hampshire.* Philadelphia: Robert Aitken, 1784.
Bicknell, Thomas W. *250th Anniversary of the Settlement of Rehoboth, Massachusetts, 1644–1894.* Printed by author, 1894.
Bodge, George M. *The Soldiers of King Philip's War.* Boston: David Clapp & Son, 1891.
Church, Benjamin. *Diary of King Philip's War, 1675–1676.* Published for the Little Compton Historical Society. Chester, CT: Pequot Press, 1975.
———. *The History of King Philip's War.* Boston: John Kimball Wiggin, 1865.
Church, Thomas, and Samuel G. Drake. *The History of the Great Indian War of 1675 and 1676 Commonly Called King Philip's War. Also, the Old French and Indian Wars from 1689 to 1704.* Hartford, CT: Silas Andrus and Son, 1852.
Clauson, J. Earl. *These Plantations.* Providence, RI: E.A. Johnson, 1937.
Cole, J.R. *History of Washington and Kent Counties, Rhode Island.* New York: Preston, 1889.
Crane, Ellory Bicknell. *Historic Homes and Institutions and Genealogical and Personal Memoirs of Worcester County Massachusetts, with a History of Worcester Society of Antiquity.* Vol. 1. New York: Lewis, 1907.

D'Agostino, Thomas, and Arlene Nicholson. *Haunted Litchfield County.* Charleston, SC: The History Press, 2020.

————. *Legends, Lore and Secrets of New England.* Charleston, SC: The History Press, 2013.

Damon, Laura. "Muskets in Misery Swamp: An Investigation into a King Philip's War Battle." Unpublished master's thesis, University of Rhode Island, 2018.

DeForest, John W. *History of the Indians of Connecticut from the Earliest Known Period to 1850.* Hartford, CT: Wm. Jas. Hammersley, 1851.

Drake, Samuel Adams. *A Book of New England Legends and Folklore in Prose and Poetry.* Boston: Little, Brown, 1910.

Easton, John. *A Narrative of the Causes Which Led to Philip's Indian War of 1675 and 1676.* Albany, NY: J. Munsell, 1868.

Ellis, George W., and John E. Morris. *King Philip's War Based on the Archives and Records of Massachusetts, Plymouth, Rhode Island and Connecticut and Contemporary Letters and Accounts.* New York: Grafton Press, 1906.

Gabrielle, Vincent, and Joshua Eaton. "How Indigenous Grave Robbing Took Hold in What's Now New England." CT Insider, March 3, 2023. https://www.ctinsider.com/news/article/indigenous-grave-robbing-new-england-17810749.php.

Gleeson, Alice Collins. *Colonial Rhode Island.* Pawtucket, RI: Automobile, 1926.

Gookin, Daniel. *Historical Account of the Doings and Sufferings of the Christian Indians in New England in the Years 1675–1677.* Whitefish, MT: Kessinger, 2003.

————. *Historical Collections of the Indians in New England.* Boston: Belknap and Hall, 1792.

Gray, T.M. *Ghosts of Maine.* Atglen, PA: Schiffer, 2008.

Holmes, Richard. *Nutfield Rambles.* Portsmouth, NH: Peter E. Randall, 2007.

Hubbard, William. *General History of New England from the Discovery to MDCLXXX.* Boston: Charles C. Little and James Brown, 1868.

————. *The History of the Indian Wars in New England from the First Settlement to the Termination of the War with King Philip in 1677.* Roxbury, MA: printed for W. Elliot Woodward, 1865.

Hughes, Patricia. *More Lost Loot: Ghostly New England Treasure Tales.* Atglen, PA: Schiffer, 2010.

Hutchinson, Thomas. *History of Massachusetts from the First Settlement Thereof in 1628 Until the Year 1750.* Salem, MA: Thomas C. Cushing, 1795.

Kimball, Gertrude Selwyn. *Providence in Colonial Times.* New York: Houghton Mifflin, 1912.

LaCroix, Henry. *Banner of Light: An Exponent of the Spiritual Philosophy of the Nineteenth Century* 37, no. 26 (September 26, 1875).

Lamothe, Zachary. *Connecticut Lore*. Atglen, PA: Schiffer, 2013.

———. *More Connecticut Lore*. Atglen, PA: Schiffer, 2016.

Larned, Ellen D. *History of Windham County Connecticut, 1600–1760*. Pomfret, CT: Swordsmith Productions, 2000.

———. *History of Windham County Connecticut, 1760–1880*. Pomfret, CT: Swordsmith Productions, 2000.

Leach, Douglar Edward. *Flintlock and Tomahawk. New England in King Philip's War*. Woodstock, VT: Countryman Press, 2009.

Lodi, Edward. *Ghosts from King Philip's War*. Middleborough, MA: Rock Village, 2006.

Lover's Leap: An Old Indian Legend Relative to the Lover's Leap, Located on the Banks of Kenduskeag Stream Opposite the Present Site of the Maxfield Plant. Bangor Special Collections, 1900.

Mather, Cotton. *Magnalia Christi Americana; or the Ecclesiastical History of New England from Its First Planting in the Year 1620, Unto the Year of Our Lord 1698*. Hartford: Silas Andrus, Roberts & Burr, 1820.

Mather, Increase. *A Brief History of the War with the Indians in New-England*. London: Rose and Crown, 1676.

McCain, Diana Ross. *Mysteries and Legends of New England*. Guilford, CT: Globe Pequot Press, 2009.

McGreen, M.E. Reilly. *Rhode Island Legends: Haunted Hallows and Monster's Lairs*. Charleston, SC: History Press, 2012.

Morton, Thomas. *New English Canaan*. Amsterdam: Jacob Frederick Stam., 1637.

Mowry, Arthur May, and William A. Mowry. *First Steps in the History of our Country*. Boston: Silver Burdett, 1898.

Olcott, Henry S. *People from the Other World*. Hartford, CT: American, 1875.

Perry, Elizabeth A. *A Brief History of the Town of Glocester Rhode Island Preceded by a Sketch of the Territory While a Part of Providence*. Providence, RI: Providence Press, 1886.

Perry, Jean. "The Mystery of the Spooky Stone Head." *Wanderer* 26, issue 42, no. 1278 (October 19, 2017).

Quest, Olga Hall. *Flames over New England: The Story of King Philip's War 1675–1676*. New York: E.P. Dutton, 1967.

Rider, Sidney S. *The Lands of Rhode Island as They Were Known to Caunounicus and Miantunnomu when Roger Williams Came in 1636*. Providence, RI: published by the author, 1904.

Rowlandson, Mary. *The Sovereignty and Goodness of God: Being a Narrative of the Captivity and Restoration of Mrs. Mary Rowlandson.* Cambridge, MA: self-published, 1682.

Schultz, Eric B., and Michael J. Tougias. *King Philip's War: The History and Legacy of America's Forgotten Conflict.* New York: Countryman Press, 1999.

Sheldon, George. *History of Deerfield, Massachusetts: The Times When and the People by Whom It Was Settled, Unsettled & Resettled.* Vol. 1. Greenfield, MA: E.A. Hall, 1895.

Simmons, William S. *The Spirit of the New England Tribes: Indian History and Folklore, 1620–1984.* Hanover, NH: University Press of New England, 1986.

Skinner, Charles Montgomery. *Myths and Legends of Our Own Land.* Philadelphia: J.P. Lippincott, 1896.

Smith-Johnson, Robin. *Legends & Lore of Cape Cod.* Charleston, SC: The History Press, 2016.

Souza, Kenneth J. "Walking Among the Dead: A Tour of Tri-Town Graveyards." *Wanderer* 2, no. 42 (October 29, 1993). Weekly publication serving Marion, Mattapoisett and Rochester, Massachusetts.

Stevens, Austin. *Mysterious New England.* Dublin, NH: Yankee, 1971.

Stiles, Ezra. *A History of Three of the Judges of King Charles I.* Hartford, CT: Elisha Babcock, 1794.

Strock, Daniel Jr. *Pictoral History of King Philip's War.* Boston: Horace Wentworth, 1851.

Sudborough, Susannah. "13 Bridgewater Triangle 'Hotspots' That Will Take You into the Unknown This Halloween." *Enterprise*, October 13, 2021.

Transactions and Collections of the American Antiquarian Society, Volume II. Cambridge, MA: University Press, 1836.

Wardwell, Hosea B. "The Traditions of the Elders." *Republican Journal* (Belfast, ME), May 21, 1885.

Waters, Thomas Franklin. *Ipswich in the Massachusetts Bay Colony.* Salem, MA: Salem Press, 1905.

White, Glenn E. *Folk Tales of Connecticut.* Meriden, CT: Journal Press, 1977.

———. *Folk Tales of Connecticut Volume II.* Meriden, CT: Journal Press, 1981.

Whittier, John Greenleaf. *The Poems of John Greenleaf Whittier.* New York: A.L. Burt, 1900.

Wilbur, Keith C. *The New England Indians.* Guilford, CT: Globe Pequot, 1978.

Williams, Roger. *A Key into the Language of America.* London: Gregory Dexter, 1643.

Other Sources

Atlas Obscura. https://www.atlasobscura.com.

Boston.com. https://www.boston.com.

Heritage History. https://www.heritage-history.com

Historical Marker Database. https://www.hmdb.org.

The Joseph Bucklin Society. http://bucklinsociety.net.

National Geographic Open Explorer. http://www.neexplorers.org

New England Historical Society. https://newenglandhistoricalsociety.com.

New England Legends Podcast. "Episode 213: The Devil and the Crying Rocks: Charlestown, Rhode Island." https://ournewenglandlegends.com/podcast-213-the-devil-and-the-crying-rocks/.

Only in Your State. https://www.onlyinyourstate.com.

Plymouth Archaeological Rediscovery Project (PARP). "Clarke Garrison House Massacre." plymoutharch.tripod.com/id16.html.

South Coast Today. https://www.southcoasttoday.com/.

Stone Wings (blog). https://stonewings.wordpress.com.

Strange New England. http://www.strange-new-england.com.

Wikipedia. https://www.wikipedia.org.

The Witchery Arts. https://www.gothichorrorstories.com.

World History Encyclopedia. https://www.worldhistory.org.

ABOUT THE AUTHORS

Thomas D'Agostino and Arlene Nicholson have been extensively studying and investigating paranormal accounts for over forty-two years with over two thousand investigations to their credit. Creators of seventeen books and counting, together they have penned and captured on film the best haunts and history New England has to offer.

The couple has appeared in many television shows, documentaries, radio shows, podcasts and publications as well as contributing to other books written by paranormal authors.

Tom is a graduate of Rhode Island College with a degree in political science. In his spare time, Tom refurbishes antique clocks and builds his own musical instruments, many from the medieval and renaissance eras.

Arlene is a professional photographer. Arlene's vast education spans from photography to marketing and fundraising. Arlene is also a talented tarot card reader with years of experience and success in the field.

Tom and Arlene work together with some of the best names in the field investigating the paranormal from New England and beyond. They are founders of Dining With the Dead 1031, an interactive paranormal investigation dinner event in some of the most haunted places in the region where guests are the investigators and use the equipment supplied or their own during the investigations.

Thomas and Arlene presently reside in Connecticut.

www.tomdagostino.com

FREE eBOOK OFFER

Scan the QR code below, enter your e-mail address and get our original Haunted America compilation eBook delivered straight to your inbox for free.

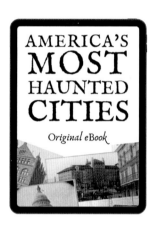

ABOUT THE BOOK

Every city, town, parish, community and school has their own paranormal history. Whether they are spirits caught in the Bardo, ancestors checking on their descendants, restless souls sending a message or simply spectral troublemakers, ghosts have been part of the human tradition from the beginning of time.

In this book, we feature a collection of stories from five of America's most haunted cities: Baltimore, Chicago, Galveston, New Orleans and Washington, D.C.

SCAN TO GET
AMERICA'S MOST HAUNTED CITIES

Having trouble scanning? Go to:
biz.arcadiapublishing.com/americas-most-haunted-cities